.

BEAR TALES &
TRAPLINE
TRAILS

True Adventures of an Oregon Woodsman

BEAR TALES & TRAPLINE TRAILS

True Adventures of an Oregon Woodsman

BOB GILMAN

PACIFIC PUBLISHING   FLORENCE • OREGON

PACIFIC PUBLISHING
FLORENCE • OREGON

Book design and composition by
Robert Serra / Pacific Publishing

Cover art by Ralph Flowers
Back cover photo by Charlie Mock

Illustrations by Sharon Davis and Ralph Flowers

Library of Congress Control Number: 2014935639
ISBN: 9780985180133

Inquiries:
Pacific Publishing
P.O. Box 2767
327 Laurel Street
Florence, OR 97439
(541) 997-1040
www.connectflorence.com

First Edition

Preface

If I were to ask four different people what happened at the same event they all attended yesterday, I would likely get four different versions of the story. And so it is with any story told. I was recently asked if all the tales in this book are true. Yes, they are as true as I can remember them. Many of these events are well documented by reports and journals that I have kept. Other events are thirty or more years old and I have attempted to recount those memories as best I can. I have little doubt, however, that in my story telling, I have occasionally shined a little brighter than I should have or remembered events differently than others would. While there may be minor discrepancies in some facts, nothing was purposely fabricated other than a couple of people's names. I have changed those names for what I hope will be obvious reasons. — *Bob Gilman*

Introduction

History has always interested me. My bookshelves are overflowing with books on the fur trade and history of Oregon. Throughout my years as a fur trapper, hunter and animal damage control agent, I have slowly gained a sense of local history about trapping, outdoor skills and knowledge of the country I grew up in. The house where I spent the first eight years of my life stood only a few feet from the Hudson's Bay Trail to the Umpqua fur country. The streams and mountains in western Oregon that I have trapped over the past fifty-plus years were first worked by John Jacob Astor's Pacific Fur Company trappers as early as 1812. I now share a common history with these first trappers and the many others who have trod these forests and streams over the last two hundred years. It only remains to put my experiences on paper for others, I hope, to enjoy. I have certainly enjoyed living the life of a trapper and woodsman.

My grandmother, Lizzie Cary Gilman, instilled in me a sense of family history, and while still in high school I began to compile some family history notes and old family pictures. Now over forty years later I have included a little of my family history in this book. While working on this project my research made me realize how little I really knew about my parents, grandparents and the extended family. That lack of knowledge of my family history prompted me to start writing this story. I determined to share some of the interesting events of my life and give my children and grandchildren a firsthand account of some of their family history.

I am also mindful that by today's standards I have pursued a unique lifestyle that is far removed from most of contemporary society. Even in this day there are plenty of trappers, many of them far more skilled at capturing animals than I. However, by pursuing this life with great enthusiasm and never doubting that it was the right course for me, I have had opportunities and experiences that are unique for this time in history, even among professional trappers. Foremost of those unique experiences has been my nearly thirty years of bear damage control as a private contractor. In those years I have privately contracted for many of the largest corporate timberland owners in Oregon.

In the accounts that follow I lay out some of the more memorable events that have shaped my life and some of the people who taught me both outdoor skills and valuable lessons over the last fifty years. Some of these people are memorable characters. Others are good friends and I would like to pass on some of the memories I have of them. Along the way I also relate some of the trapping history of the country I have grown up and worked in since April 6, 1950, when I started the journey of life.

I decided on the profession of a trapper at a very early age. I was five years old in 1955 when our family at Mill Camp near the small community of Lorane, Oregon, had a visit from a wilderness trapper from British Columbia. Kenneth Raymond, a cousin of my dad, had spent the winter of 1951 with this trapper on his wilderness trapline east of Bella Coola, British Columbia. A few years later the trapper came south to Oregon to visit Kenneth and they in turn came to visit my family at our Mill Camp home. I have only a vague memory of some grizzly bear and trapping stories that he related to us.

In later years when I asked dad about this visit he couldn't remember the trapper's name or even where in B.C. the trapping took place. After this visit I went over to my best friend Walter Lacky's house, and I clearly remember telling him that I had decided to become a wilderness trapper. I doubt that I really understood at the time what a wilderness trapper did but it must have sounded very exciting. A seed was planted that never left my mind, and all through my adolescent years I dreamed about someday becoming a trapper.

That trapper from British Columbia would have had no idea what a profound impact his visit had on my life. It was nearly fifty-five years before I found out who this trapper was and precisely where he came from. His name was Bob Ratcliff, and if my research is correct, the Ratcliff family was originally from Oregon and had migrated to British Columbia. In 1950 they lived east of Bella Coola, British Columbia, in a little community called Atnarko. I found information about the Ratcliff family in two publications about the Bella Coola area. References about the family were found in *Ruffles on My Long Johns* by Isabel Edwards written in 1980. A story about Bob Ratcliff also appears in a book called *White Guys and Grizzlies: The Story of Clayton Mack* compiled and edited by Harvey Thommasen in 1993.

The Ratcliff men were true wilderness trappers and I suspect they passed on their heritage to many young men. The seed planted by Bob Ratcliff was a small one indeed but it took root in my mind and has continued to grow throughout my life. I never left Oregon for the far north wilderness, however, many exciting adventures lay before me in the wild and untamed areas of the Oregon outback.

Several old-time Oregon hunters and trappers have impacted and helped to shape my life. Wayne Negus was a famous Oregon trapper who first instructed me in what turned out to be a lifelong obsession with the American marten. Joe Jackson was not as well known as Wayne, but he was a skilled cougar hunter and outdoorsman of an earlier era. Joe showed me my first lion track when I was fourteen years old as we hunted for elk on the Grand Ronde River breaks of northeastern Oregon. Joe's story telling around many campfires was an education in and of itself. Ralph Flowers, without question one of the greatest bear hunter/trappers of all time, was my friend and

mentor. Ralph impacted my life in many ways. He taught me valuable skills and shared his tremendous knowledge about black bears
and damage control, but no less important was his example of moral
character. I hope to relate just a little about these and others who
travelled the same paths as I. Oregon has a rich trapping history. I've
done my best to capture a small piece of that in these stories.

Inspiration for this book came from family. My hope is that along
with entertainment this book educates my grandchildren, family and
others about the unique life I have been blessed to lead. I hope to
inform trappers and other outdoorsmen in some little subject that
they may have missed. I hope to teach just a little to those who have
far more academic education than I about what the trapping lifestyle
really is. A trapper's life is much different than the caricature cre-
ated by the animal rights activists. Lastly, as a completely amateur
historian, I would like to add a few lines to the history of trapping
in Oregon. I hope that family, friends, outdoorsmen or others who
read these stories will come away with a sense of who I am, and by
extension will become acquainted with the trapper's lifestyle and
why we so passionately pursue this way of life.

A number of years ago, my wife found a little framed copy of the
following quote from President Calvin Coolidge. She thought that it
pretty well summed up how I have lived my life:

*Nothing in this world can take the place of persistence. Talent will
not; nothing is more common than unsuccessful people with talent. Genius will not; unrewarded genius is almost a proverb. Education will not; the world is full of educated derelicts. Persistence
and determination alone are omnipotent. The slogan "press on"
has solved and always will solve the problems of the human race.*

Calvin Coolidge, 30th President of the United States, 1872-1933

Acknowledgments

In attempting to tell life stories that have accumulated over sixty years, it becomes clear that even an outdoorsman who is well satisfied with his own company interacts with a pile of other individuals. In these stories, I have written not only of my personal adventures, but in many cases have included friends, employees, family or acquaintances I have met along the paths of life. I give them all full credit for weaving the fabric that makes life interesting and, I hope, some small adventures worth telling.

For most of my life I did not aspire to be an author, so it took inspiration to start down this path and even more inspiration to complete the work. For this, all the credit goes to my grandchildren. It is for them that I have written this book. I hope through this book to share with them significant memories of my life.

For a student who frequently did not show up to high school classes and avoided formal education at all cost, to write a book takes a lot of help. It is, of course, not possible to mention all who have contributed in diverse ways, both large and small. Nevertheless, I must try and give an accounting of some who were instrumental in any positive attributes of this final product.

Tom Krause, former editor of *The American Trapper* magazine, accepted my first article for publication during 2007. With credit to Tom's editing abilities, my very first article, "Trapline Hazards" in the summer 2007 edition of *The American Trapper*, was chosen as best unsolicited article of the year. Tom has influenced my writing in many ways. His articles, books and videos are among the best, and his leadership on national issues as an advocate for trappers is matched by few.

Bob Noonan, publisher of the *Trapper's Post* magazine, has been helpful with valuable advice in the daunting task of producing a first book. Bob connected me with the talented illustrator Sharon Davis. Sharon produces art and drawings for *The Trapper's Post* and *Fur-Fish-Game* magazines. She also does illustrations and art work for books, and some of her work will be found in this book. She can be contacted through her website at *http://www.illustrationsinmotion.com*.

Thanks to Sally-Jo Bowman, friend, writer and editor who first read the draft manuscript, urged me to tell my story and continued to give me encouragement throughout the process. Thanks to David Walp for his influence and friendship. Thanks to Tamara Moan for editing the original manuscript and cheerfully working with someone who didn't know and still doesn't know what he was doing.

Thanks to Gary Blanchard, who worked for Starker Forests Inc., of Corvallis, Oregon, for fifty-two years and served as Chief Forester for that company from 1971 until 2008. Gary's enthusiasm for the manuscript, his corrections, general input and friendship is very much appreciated.

Thanks to Ralph Flowers' daughters, Sylvan and Jackie, for graciously allowing me free use of Ralph's art work for this publication. Sylvan may be contacted at *pacelich@q.com* for more information about Ralph's art and books.

Thanks also to Wesley Murphey, trapper, author, former employee and friend who has reviewed the draft manuscript, given good advice and been very helpful about how to write and publish a book.

Special thanks to Tim Hiller, Tom Krause, Gerald Schmitt, Bob Dick and Georg Ziegltrum for reviewing, correcting and commenting on the final manuscript.

I am greatly indebted to the numerous foresters I have worked for over these many years of contracting. They were in reality my bosses, but I have always considered them my friends.

Table of Contents

Rebels, Feuds and Cowboys	1
A Boy and the Outdoors	5
Mike and the Trapping Bug	12
Down the Siuslaw	16
Lanterns and Flat-Tails	22
Big Game and Bear Hunting	25
Cliff and the Poachers	30
Romance, Marriage and the Dreadful Sawmill	34
The Art of Tracking	41
The Dog Man and the Trapper	49
Cat Skull Camp	60
Hungry for Pancakes	63
Ever Seen Bigfoot?	67
High-Flying Saucers?	69
Getting to Know Big Jim	71
Trapline Hazards and the Big Wind of '81	73
Deadfalls are Dangerous!	76
Willamette Canoe Lines	80
Weekly — Not Daily!	82
A Fragrant Christmas Tree	86
Cascade Marten Lines	88

Boomers by the Hundreds   101

We All Make Mistakes   107

1980 Campaign "The Cost of Freedom"   113

A Partner and Boomers by the Thousands   117

I'll Make a Woman Out of You!   119

Then Came the Bears   122

The Washington "Bear Man"   125

The Alsea Bear Job   130

The Coast Range Bear Study   142

The Professor and Me   146

Ike and the Howling Bears   152

Scott Takes a Turkey   156

In the Christmas Spirit   157

Draggin' Beaver   160

The Big Cats   165

Axe Handles and Ex-Cons   175

Favorite Hunts   185

Charlie in Survival Mode   203

Tribute to a Partner   212

The Bear Trappers   220

Final Thoughts   240

The Author   242

Bibliography   244

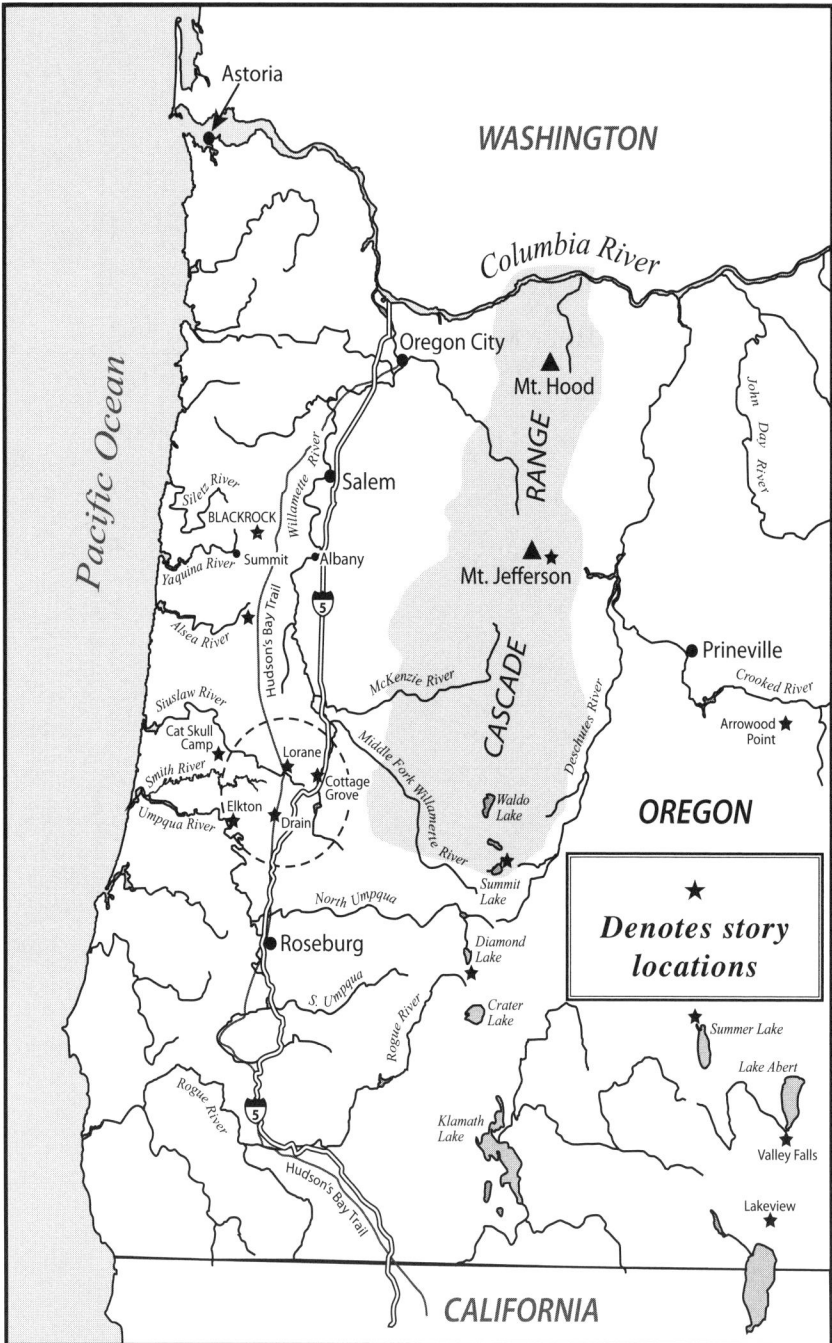

Pacific Ocean

WASHINGTON

Astoria

Columbia River

Oregon City

▲ Mt. Hood

Salem

Siletz River

BLACKROCK

Willamette River

Yaquina River Summit Albany

RANGE

▲★ Mt. Jefferson

John Day River

Alsea River

Hudson's Bay Trail

5

McKenzie River

CASCADE

Deschutes River

● Prineville

Crooked River

Arrowood ★
Point

Siuslaw River

Cat Skull
Camp ★

Lorane

Middle Fork Willamette River

Smith River Elkton Cottage
Grove

Umpqua River Drain

*Waldo
Lake*

OREGON

North Umpqua

★ *Summit
Lake*

*Diamond
Lake* ★

● Roseburg

S. Umpqua

Rogue River

*Crater
Lake*

★ *Summer Lake*

Lake Abert

5

Rogue River

*Klamath
Lake*

★
Valley Falls

Hudson's Bay Trail

Lakeview
★

★

***Denotes story
locations***

CALIFORNIA

The Gilman and Murray clans at Murray Ranch, Grassy Butte, North Dakota on the Fourth of July, 1911. Sam and Lizzie Gilman, back row, far right; Ab Murray, front row, side view.

Rebels, Feuds and Cowboys

A Brief Family History

My grandmother Lizzie came to Drain, Oregon, in 1904 with her parents, George Hense and Mintie Cary, and my second great grandparents, William Cary and Patsy Cline Cary. In 1910 Lizzie went to North Dakota to visit relatives and married Sam Gilman. The Gilmans and Carys had been in-laws since right after the Civil War when they met up near Kingston, Minnesota, in 1865.

It appears that my second great-grandfather, William Cary, probably deserted the Confederate army and may have had good reason for leaving West Virginia and heading north before the end of the war. William had been a neighbor of "Devil" Anse Hatfield and served with him and the Logan County Wildcats during the Civil

1

Great Grandparents Hense and Mintin Cary and their sons (from left): Fred, Bill and Elmer. Elizabeth Dewey is three years old. Bertha, Minnesota, 1890.

War. William's wife, Patsy Cline Cary, was daughter of "Alum" Billy (William) Cline of Alum Creek on the Tug Fork of the Big Sandy River in Logan County West Virginia.

The Clines were also neighbors with both the Hatfields and McCoys. The feud between these families may have started during the Civil War and it is probable that Will Cary and Patsy Cline Cary were affected by the beginnings of this feud. The Carys and several other families left West Virginia for Oregon in 1864, but according to family remembrances were sidetracked off the Oregon Trail.

The Gilman and Cary families met in southern Minnesota in 1865 where both families settled for the next nineteen years. The Cary family settled near Bertha, and the Gilman clan near Kingston on the north end of Swan Lake. The Gilmans then moved on to North Dakota and the Carys again headed for Oregon.

My grandpa, Sam Gilman, came to North Dakota in 1885 when he was six years old and grew up around Belfield and Dickenson. Grandpa Sam's dad, brothers and later brothers-in-law became horse and cattle ranchers who owned small ranches near Grassy Butte, North Dakota. Ab Murray married Dillie Gilman and became Sam's brother-in-law. Ab's grandson, Cecil Murray, still owns the original Murray family homestead in the Grassy Butte area.

After Sam and Lizzie were married in 1911, Sam sold his horse and cattle holdings and they moved on to Drain. A few years later Grandpa traded his house in Drain to his brother-in-law, John Albert (Bert) DeLaunay, for a small ranch on Bear Creek near Curtin just a few miles north of Drain.

My dad, Don Gilman, was born in Drain and grew up on the small 140-acre "ranch" that Grandpa Sam owned on North Bear Creek, 1.5 miles east of Curtin. As young boys during the Great Depression, Don and his brother, Howard, roamed the hills for several miles around. Ward's and Horn's Buttes were the prominent landmarks and the destination for many early hunting and camping excursions. Through the years the boys became skilled hunters who helped keep the family larder filled during the Depression years. In that early time, the mountains surrounding the ranch were covered with virgin old growth forest where blue grouse thrived in unbelievable numbers and deer and grouse were a primary source of meat in the lean years. Fishing, hunting and farm chores dominated their boyhood years in the 1930s.

The idyllic boyhood years during the Great Depression changed dramatically for Howard and Don on December 7, 1942, when the Japanese attacked Pearl Harbor. World War II would dominate their lives for the next several years. Howard served in the European theater and Don served in the South Pacific. When the war was over the Gilman brothers returned home and took up life where they had left off. Guns came out of storage, got cleaned, oiled and put back into

3

use. Hunting and fishing would be their primary outdoor activities for the rest of their lives.

After he married Barbara Ware and settled at Mill Camp on Sandy Creek near the headwaters of the Siuslaw River, Dad and Mom began passing on that hunting legacy to me as I grew into a young boy during the early 1950s.

Black Bear illustration by Ralph Flowers

A Boy and the Outdoors

Some of my first memories are of fishing and hunting excursions with my dad and mom, Don and Barbara Gilman. At five years old I remember trailing along behind Dad as he shot a good four point (western count) blacktail buck. We were in the tall bracken fern patches in the hills along the Siuslaw River drainage a few miles below Lorane in the Coast Range Mountains of western Oregon.

Another early memory is of Dad and me catching small native cutthroat trout in Pass Creek near Curtin near where Dad grew up. This tiny shaded stream with moss covered rocks and abundant stands of red alder was at that time alive with the bright little fish that wiggled magically up out of the pool. I must have been about four or five years old on that short fishing trip, but the memory of those shiny little fish is as clear as that mountain stream. In the next fifty years I would fish in dozens of small and large streams throughout Oregon and other states. Hunting trips for deer, bear and elk would become an inseparable part of my life. I was ten years old when trapping for muskrats and beaver started me on a lifelong adventure. The die was cast for me at a very early age.

Dad was not the only hunter in our family. Mom didn't have much experience hunting before she married Dad but she was a quick study. Hunting and fishing soon became a significant part of her life. Her old worn 30-30 Winchester rifle has dropped dozens of blacktail bucks over the years. Mom's 348 Winchester lever action rifle has also downed numerous bull elk. When it came to fishing Mom never wanted to quit. It was always just one more fish or one more pass around the lake until Dad became exasperated. Mom's

5

Barbara and Don Gilman, Lakeview, Oregon area, 1946.

attitude of never giving up while hunting and fishing was a lesson I learned well. Eighty-two years old in 2010, Barbara Gilman spent the entire deer season in eastern Oregon camping and hunting with as much enthusiasm as ever.

In the early 1950s, dad began working for the Rickini Lumber Company sawmill at Saginaw. He worked long hours and commuted from our simple house at Mill Camp that was situated three miles south of the little community of Lorane. In the 1940s, many small communities had grown up around small sawmills that eventually shut down after the easily accessible timber was cut. Mill Camp was such a community with about twenty mill houses left over from the boom days of the two sawmills on Sandy Creek. Mill Camp was located on an upper tributary of the Siuslaw River drainage, right on Territorial Road, that in the 1820s and '30s, had been one of the Hudson's Bay trails into the Umpqua fur country. On June 5, 1834, John Work's Hudson's Bay trapping brigade camped on the Siuslaw (Yangama River) at the north side of Elk Mountain. Work's journal gives a detailed description of the trail and the surrounding land-scape where the little communities of Lorane and Mill Camp would eventually be established.

Hudson's Bay trappers had started taking beaver from the Si-uslaw and its tributaries in the mid-1820s. Since that time, numerous trappers have worked the Siuslaw, Umpqua, Smith and other coastal streams for beaver and other furs. Starting in the 1960s, I became one of those trappers. The headwaters of the Siuslaw drainage just over the hill from the Umpqua drainage became the foundation of my lifelong career as a trapper.

Heading south from Mill Camp, the Hudson's Bay Trail went over a low divide the trappers called Elk Mountain, and within two miles dropped into the Umpqua River tributary of Pheasant Creek. Following down Pheasant Creek on today's road for about three miles leads to the confluence with Pass Creek at the little community of Anlauf. From there the old trail follows Pass Creek and intersects Elk Creek at Drain. Heading west from the current Drain, within four miles the valley opens up into a lush rolling hills landscape. This little secluded valley was a prime camping location for those early trapping brigades with good feed for the horses and abundant wood and water close by.

Today a few scattered rural houses and farms dot this beauti-ful Coast Range valley and an old Grange hall called Sunnydale gives the valley its current name. In earlier years this valley had been called Tin Pot, a name which according to one story originated from a pack animal having a wreck and scattering pots and pans down the pack trail.

In the fall of 1849, Jesse Applegate and his son-in-law, Charles Putnam, rode from Jesse's donation land claim near Yoncalla over to Tin Pot Valley where Jesse thought Charles might like to stake his claim. The ride down Elk Creek was "marked by the brilliant scarlet of the vine maple, the yellow of the broad-leaf maple the golden brown of the ash and here and there the red-pink leaves of autumn dogwood." When Jesse Applegate and Charles Putnam broke out into the open grass-covered valley, Charles knew he had found his home. Few places in western Oregon can match the beauty of this little valley.

Charles Putnam lived the rest of his life at Tin Pot and several generations of his family and friends are now buried in the little private Putnam Cemetery on the original donation land claim a little west of the Sunnydale Grange and on the south side of Highway 38. Among those graves are several generations of my family, both Gilman and Cary, along with numerous other relatives including the Lowe, Raymond, DeLaunay and Montgomery families.

Civil War veteran William Cary and his wife, Patsy Cline Cary, my second great grandparents, are buried here in unmarked graves. Great-Grandparents George Hense and Mintin Cary are also laid to rest nearby. My grandparents, Sam and Lizzie Gilman, and their sons, Merwin, Howard and my father, Donald, are also buried in this special little Coast Range valley. My family had started this journey to Tin Pot from the hills of West Virginia and the lake country of Minnesota to the prairies of North Dakota. From there they made stops and left roots in Montana and Idaho before moving on to western Oregon.

In the 1820s through the 1840s, many Hudson's Bay trapping brigades passed through this valley and many famous trappers built their campfires and roasted their suppers near where my family rests. Men like McKay, Gervais, Desportes, Gagnier, LaBonte, Lucier and others set their beaver traps in Elk Creek and other nearby tributaries of the Umpqua and Smith rivers and my favorite river drainage, the Siuslaw. I started my life just a few miles from this little valley and hope to finish it at this location surrounded by family and resting near the footprints of the trappers, woodsmen, explorers and pioneers I have so admired.

The Siuslaw River, from its headwaters downstream to Richardson, just above Mapleton where my Grandpa Ware lived for nearly forty years, played a major role in my development as a hunter, fisherman and trapper. Along the way I met a few of the old-time trappers who worked the Siuslaw country, some as early as the 1920s. I learned to love and respect this country that teemed with trout, salmon, bear, beaver, grouse, cougar, bobcats and coyotes. Eventually, I developed skills at trapping that allowed me to make a comfortable livelihood by trapping for furs and doing animal damage control trapping for livestock and agricultural damage. The outdoor lessons my folks and family taught me by example and training helped bring good success and great satisfaction to my life.

When I was in the fourth grade, Mom and Dad decided to move into the small town of Cottage Grove to be closer to work. Dad was working six days a week at Rickini sawmill and I am sure they were looking to move up in the world. I can still remember the terror I felt about moving into town. My best friend and next-door neighbor Mike Lacky, along with his sisters, began to tease me about being a "city slicker." I hated everything about moving into town, but at eight years old you don't have many choices about where you are going to live. I dreaded the thought of leaving my best friend and familiar surroundings. At this young age I had already learned to love Mill Camp and the rural areas on the upper Siuslaw River. Throughout my life I have always remembered where I came from in the small rural community at Addison Mill Camp on Sandy Creek and Territorial Road.

In the early 1960s, our family began to develop a pattern of spring and summer fishing and fall hunting vacations. Dad bought an old wooden fourteen-foot boat and we started making fishing trips to Diamond Lake and other high Cascade Mountain lakes. We often brought home coolers full of snow-packed rainbow trout. Mom usually caught the most fish and she could never seem to get enough fishing done from daylight to dark. We also fished for "stripers" (striped bass) in the lower Umpqua River at Reedsport.

We would get up at about 2:00 a.m., drive the seventy-five miles and be fishing before daylight. The Umpqua was also alive with sturgeon at this time and when the season re-opened after being closed for several years we began to take them. On the first day of legal sturgeon fishing, I landed three sturgeons that were all over five feet long, longer than I was at the time. Like many other rural families, our family used the fish and game along with other natural resources of the country to the fullest.

In the fall, hunting for deer was always our main activity. When Mom and Dad weren't working on weekends they were hunting and they usually brought me along to share the experience. We often hunted with the Black Family from Curtin along with other friends and family members. A big bunch of us would go down the Siuslaw to hunt the logged-over lands where the deer were thick. We rarely came home without deer. Mom and Dad always seemed to be among the lucky ones. I can still remember the wonderful smell of fresh venison hanging in our garage fruit room.

As Dad added up years in the Rickini sawmill, he gained a paid vacation and we would sometimes go to eastern Oregon to hunt mule deer. I made my first trip to Lakeview in south central Oregon when I was about five years old. It was on that trip I got my first smell of sagebrush and my first look at mule deer.

In my early years of hunting eastern Oregon, it was not at all

Don and Bob Gilman with sturgeon in 1960

unusual to see more than a hundred deer in a day. When I entered junior high school Mom and Dad started going on an annual elk hunt in the Lookout Mountain area near Elgin. Every year until I graduated high school I skipped school for a week of elk hunting. It didn't do my grades much good but it did wonders for my continuing outdoor education.

Mike and the Trapping Bug

Nineteen-sixty-one was an eventful year. I was eleven years old and in the sixth grade. That was the year Mom and Dad purchased a new house in Oak Park in Cottage Grove. Oak Park was a new subdivision on the very edge of town. Our new house was right on the edge (as far as I was concerned) of where the wilderness started. Hundreds of acres of uninhabited brush rows and grass fields were only a few feet beyond our back door. Blue jays, robins, wrens and other songbirds seemed to cry out constantly for me to hunt them with my trusty Daisy BB gun. I spent hundreds of hours over the next three or four years stalking this small quarry and honing my hunting and shooting skills. China pheasants were also numerous but just a little out of my class at the time. Raccoon tracks lined the ditch that bordered our yard and the fields beyond. These tracks fascinated me from the first time I observed them.

I also fell in love about this time with a pretty young girl in my sixth grade class named Christy Bush. My love for Christy was pretty much a one-sided affair. Well, now that I think about it, it was actually a completely one-sided affair. Christy was the first and last girl ever to slap me silly. I think I had made some smart remark to get her attention and I must have succeeded. I sometimes think I can still feel that slap today. She sure didn't hold back!

All was not in vain, however, since my trailing of Christy led me to find out that she had a brother named Mike. Mike and I soon became best friends and we both shared a love of the outdoors, primarily hunting and fishing. Mike was also the key to something I had been dreaming about but had never put into action. Mike's dad,

Cliff, had been a trapper at one time and Mike had possession of a few old rusty traps. We soon developed what little information we had about trapping into plans for capturing some of the local muskrats. Trapping was about to turn from just a dream into a reality. In those days we almost always walked or rode our bicycles to school and back during good weather. The shortest path from school to home lay through the old Chambers Mill that had once been a big operation in Cottage Grove, but had burned down many years before. That mill site is near where the Cottage Grove fire department stands today.

The old log pond for this mill still had about an acre of water, mostly about two feet deep and grown up in cattails. Somehow Mike knew what muskrat feed beds looked like and in the cattails were numerous feed beds. On a Saturday morning in late November of 1961, Mike and I each set two or three traps on these floating vegetation piles where the muskrats were feeding. The next morning we arrived early to check our traps and to our great astonishment found we had actually each captured a muskrat. The feel of that soft silky fur and the sweet smell of musk were overpowering, and the thought that the fur might be worth as much as a dollar was almost more than I could take.

I don't remember what Mike did but I headed for home as fast as my bicycle could carry me. Rushing into the house yelling for Mom, I found her still asleep in bed. I guess she was not nearly as excited as I was about the wet rat — held by its tail over her face just as she opened her eyes. I quickly exited the bedroom. We ended up catching fourteen muskrats from that pond and I was hooked for life. From then on trapping was my number-one thought in the winter months.

A few weeks later, Mike and I set a couple of mink traps behind his house on Cottage Grove's West Main Street. Silk Creek ran right behind his house so it naturally turned into one of our traplines.

The Mink Fights Back! Illustration by Sharon Davis

Mike's dad, Cliff, had owned a small mink farm for a short time. Mike had once observed him at pelting time euthanizing the mink. One morning we went to check our traps and with untold excitement discovered that Mike had caught a small mink. If you can imagine Patrick McManus' friend, "Crazy Eddie," you will have a fairly clear assessment of my friend, Mike Bush, in those days.

With great bravado Mike informed me that he would now demonstrate how mink trappers could quickly dispatch a live mink. Reaching for the small female, he grasped her behind the head and was about to carry out the deed, but Mike had not figured on the mink fighting back. With lightning speed the mink twisted around and sunk its teeth into Mike's knuckle! What followed was one of the funniest Indian dances complete with shrieks and war whoops that I ever observed. We eventually finished off the mink with a handy stick. Mike never again tried to break the neck of a live mink, although I did on numerous occasions observe that same bravado lead to some small disaster.

Years later in the 1990s, Mike had moved his family to Klawock, Alaska, and I went there with some friends on a fishing trip. A few days after our arrival, Mike took me on a shrimp trapping expedition about thirty miles up through the islands south of Craig. Mike had not been to this area before and we had some difficulty locating the channel from our small photocopied map. The small islands squeezed close together in an area called the Tlevac Narrows, locally known as "The Chuck."

A strong outgoing tide produced some very troubling currents. Suddenly, right in front of the boat, the water looked very much like a small waterfall where two currents collided. Mike slowed the Boston Whaler to an idle as we watched the end of a twenty-inch diameter log of unknown length pop straight up out of the water a few feet in front of the boat. I was pretty intimidated by the treacherous look of this place and would have been even more fearful had I noticed the old grave marker on shore, or known of the many native people who had drowned in that very spot over the years.

Mike looked at me and coolly assessed that we probably could make it okay. He had the exact same look on his face as he did when he was twelve years old and confidently told me it wouldn't have any effect at all as we prepared to pee on the electric fence! I began to pray as Mike moved the throttle ahead and the boat began to move. We made it just fine but I don't know if it was the prayer or if we were just lucky like the time when the electric fence was turned off. One way or the other I was pretty sure that my friend Mike hadn't changed much over the last forty years.

Grandpa John Ware (right) and neighbor Chart Richardson at Richardson on the Siuslaw River in 1981 display Bob Gilman's catch.

Down the Siuslaw

Something happened in early 1961 when I was eleven years old that would jump-start my future career as a trapper. Mom and Dad, my sister, Connie, and I went down the river to visit my grandparents, John and Cathy Ware.

Grandpa Ware had a profound impact on my life. John Henry Ware grew up in a rough and tumble family in the little town of

Omaha, Arkansas. The Wares were a large family of long standing around Omaha where they had migrated from near Chillicothe, Missouri, in 1886.

My second great grandfather, Alexander Clinton Ware, had served in the Missouri State Guard in the War of Rebellion, and Grandpa proudly referred to him as a "bushwhacker." Civil War records of Clint Ware being arrested in northwest Missouri without proper papers and spending time in a prison camp charged as a bushwhacker bear that story out. The area around Springhill in northwest Missouri where the Ware's lived was well known for the activities of anti-Union southern sympathizers.

Grandpa also told me on numerous occasions that his great-grandmother, Mary Magdalene Boone, was a cousin to Daniel Boone. Genealogy records have confirmed Grandpa's stories and reveal that Daniel Boone is my cousin seven generations removed. The Boone blood that flows in my veins is mighty thin, but even so, it was Daniel Boone and my desire to imitate the great frontiersman that helped me to harvest my first bear in my early years of hunting. Everyone knows that slim relationship isn't significant, but tell that to a fourteen-year-old boy who imagines Daniel as his close relative! Like many other young boys of my generation my heroes at the time were Daniel Boone, Davy Crockett and multiple famous cowboys.

The Wares lived down the Siuslaw River about fifty miles from Lorane and we always referred to where they lived as "down the river." From my point of view many good things were "down the river:" hunting, fishing, trapping, berry picking, wood cutting and almost anything else that seemed good to me. Right where the Siuslaw River crosses Highway 126 was another little mill camp named Austa. At one time numerous mill houses and a service station had been located there, but in 1961 only two houses were still there. In one of these houses lived my mom's Uncle Homer and

17

Aunt Frankie. Frankie was my Grandpa John Ware's sister. On the way to Grandpa's that day, we decided to stop and visit with Frankie and Homer.

Great-Uncle Homer Foster was an American Indian and a good hunter, fisherman, and unknown to me until that day, a trapper. As we arrived, my cousin, Ralph, who was a couple of years older than I, was fleshing a beaver next to the wood stove in the living room. The beaver skin was tacked out with nails in a beautiful round pattern and the flesh was scraped away from the skin leaving a nearly white leather side of the hide. The smell of fresh-skinned beaver and castor from the scent glands permeated the small house.

I was mesmerized by the deft knife swipes as Cousin Ralph fleshed that beaver with great skill. Homer and Ralph had been out trapping along the Siuslaw and had so far captured over forty beaver that season. They had sold some of them to Sol Rubin Fur Company in Seattle for over twenty dollars each. Out in the woodshed I got my first look at a whole river beaver. Five of the huge rodents, with large webbed feet, flat scaly tails and long, soft, dark brown fur, lay waiting to be skinned.

With a vision of huge piles of valuable beaver pelts in my mind, I immediately began to ask questions about how to catch these animals. Homer patiently described how and where to set beaver traps. Included in his instructions was the use of beaver lure. I had never heard of beaver lure, which he informed me is made from the castor glands of the beaver along with several secret ingredients known only to expert trappers. Homer happened to have a gallon jug of this sweet-smelling lure, or medicine, as the old-time trappers called it. I wanted to know how to make this concoction, but Homer explained that he had obtained the recipe at a great effort and cost from an old-time Siuslaw trapper named Roy Thurman. He wouldn't tell me how to make the lure but supplied me with all I needed until he died in a car accident near Mapleton a few years later.

Bob Gilman stands with results of his trapline.

Ralph eventually moved to Montana and I waited for nearly thirty-five years to learn the ingredients for this lure. When Ralph returned to the Siuslaw area, he was able to find some old scraps of paper with the recipe and gave them to me. Finally I was able to make that fine old beaver lure for myself. I still have Uncle Homer's handwritten notes of the recipe and continue to use that lure to catch beaver today.

Fifty years has not blurred the vision of those slick brown beaver my eyes first fell upon, and since that time many high stacks of beaver pelts have been harvested from my traplines. For nearly twenty years I ran traplines on a fifty-mile stretch of the Siuslaw River. Many beaver would come from the same locations where Uncle Homer had set his traps many years before. After my first lessons on beaver trapping from Homer, the fever to catch beaver never left me alone.

From the small community of Lorane near the headwaters of

the Siuslaw River, downstream for about fifty miles to where the Siuslaw crosses under Highway 126 or Route F as it was formerly called, the Siuslaw river drainage is primarily an uninhabited area. For the first few miles below Lorane a few small old mill camps, farms and houses stand, but after ten miles or so it turns into mostly vacant timberlands. Private timber companies and the BLM (Bureau of Land Management) have large holdings and there are few small private owners in that fifty-mile stretch.

Timber harvest from private and public lands has dominated the landscape over this vast area of the Oregon Coast Range Mountains since the late 1800s and early 1900s, when homesteaders and early loggers started to harvest timber along the easily assessable areas of the river valley and its tributaries. Early homesteaders used screw jacks and oxen to remove the huge old growth logs to clear land for pastures and later to market logs for cash income. Logs were rolled into the river to float down to mills located down in tidewater.

In the early 1960s, the visible remnants of old homesteads were found in numerous locations all along the upper Siuslaw valley, from Highway 126 up to the very headwaters of the Siuslaw. Most private holders of these lands eventually sold out to timber companies. By the 1980s, almost all of these old sites had been planted with fast-growing Douglas fir timber and most traces of these early home-steaders had been erased. My Dad and Uncle Howard had helped harvest timber in the early 1940s when they felled and bucked timber with crosscut saws or "misery whips," as they were often called, on the upper reaches of the Siuslaw drainage, downstream from the little community of Lorane.

With almost no regulations on timber harvest and the use of the new gas-powered saws in the 1940s, large tracts of land along the river flats and tributary streams of the Siuslaw were stripped of timber. The land was then left to reproduce on its own with the landscape dramatically altered from its original huge old-growth fir forests that grew right down to the river bank. Instead of shaded rainforest, the river banks and many tributaries were opened up to the sunlight and brush grew up along the streams. Alder, hazel, willow, vine maple, cherry, cascara and other small hardwood trees and brush replaced the giant and dense forests of the past in many areas.

Heavy timber harvest continued into the 1980s when forest cutting regulations started to change dramatically. Vast areas along the Siuslaw had changed from dense forest habitat best suited for mink, marten and otter, to an open cut-over habitat where many species of wildlife could live and survive in huge numbers. The deer, bear, elk, predator and furbearer populations exploded after logging much like they do a few years after a large wildfire. Beaver were among the greatest beneficiaries of the new landscape.

In the early 1930s, just when some of the tributary streams along the Siuslaw drainage had begun turning into superb beaver habitat, something happened that helped the river beaver population increase dramatically, not only in the Siuslaw drainage but also in many other areas of the Oregon Coast Range mountains. River beaver had been trapped to very low levels by the old-time fur trappers. In 1932, the Oregon State Game Commission closed beaver trapping and started a beaver reintroduction project. Beaver were live-trapped in areas where they were more plentiful, like the Willamette Valley, then transplanted into the Coast Range streams.

The Siuslaw had very few beaver in those days, but with the habitat change and the new beavers seeded into many of the small tributaries, the Siuslaw beaver population began to grow. By the time I started trapping beavers in 1960, almost every tributary had extensive beaver colonies. The main Siuslaw River itself was also excellent habitat and well stocked with beaver. The river had excellent runs of steelhead, silvers, Chinook and sea-run cutthroats which helped to maintain a healthy otter population.

Al Weekly was one of the state trappers who trapped and

transplanted beavers into the Siuslaw drainage in the early 1940s. I didn't get to know Al until almost forty years after he had planted beavers on Buck Creek, Doe Creek and other tributaries of the Siuslaw and other coastal rivers. He had just turned eighty when I first met him and was still trapping some of the same colonies he had helped establish some forty years before.

As I turned eleven years old in 1961, the stage was set for the traplines that I would run along the Siuslaw River and its tributaries for the next twenty-plus years.

Lanterns and Flat-Tails

In 1961, we lived in Cottage Grove in the upper Willamette Valley about five miles over the mountain from the headwaters of the Siuslaw River. Dad was working long hours six days a week pulling lumber on the planer chain at the Rickini Lumber Company Sawmill. I was determined to trap beaver that winter and had badgered Dad into buying a trapping license since I was not old enough. Dad tried to persuade me to not become a beaver trapper, but to no avail, and he finally gave in. I suspect he was thinking that my trapline might cause him some extra work, since the only beaver ponds that we knew about at the time were some thirty miles away. He was right.

In the fall of that year we had hunted as usual down the river a few miles below Lorane. About six or seven miles from the Lorane store was an old homestead where only the apple orchard remained as evidence of the hard work of some homesteader of years gone by. At this old site, two logs still spanned the river where a logging bridge had once crossed. On the other side of the river the abandoned road wound for three or four miles up a small tributary stream and on up the mountain where we had made numerous deer drives that fall.

Along the road that followed the creek were numerous beaver dams with fresh yellow sticks that beavers had recently peeled and muddy beaver trails leading up the banks into the surrounding vegetation.

One Sunday in early winter, Dad and I drove over the mountain to Lorane and then down the river to the old homestead. After parking the truck we loaded up half a dozen No. 3 longspring Victor traps, wire and beaver lure. We crossed the river which was about fifty feet wide at that point and started walking up the old overgrown logging road. About a mile-and-a-half up the canyon we arrived at the beaver ponds.

We then started setting our traps and wiring them off to alder trees. We added a little beaver lure near each trap following Homer's instructions, and in a couple of hours we were hiking back down the canyon and headed for home. Uncle Homer had given strict instructions on rigging a slide-wire drowning setup to automatically dispatch the beaver when it stepped in the trap. Dad and I discussed this, but decided it was not really necessary and just tied our traps directly to some large alder trees. This was a big mistake. When we returned later we found two beaver had escaped from traps and another trap missing completely. This was one of the many hard lessons learned early in my trapping education. From that time forward I always used a humane drowning set-up or kill-type traps to capture beaver.

I had not thought the whole process through but soon realized on Tuesday evening after Dad got off work that it would be dark before we arrived at our beaver ponds. This was just one of many times that Dad did something to help me learn to take care of myself and to support my plans. It must have been difficult for him to spend his day off taking me to set traps and then return to check them twice a week when we didn't get home until after 10:00 p.m. But he never had a word of complaint. He and Mom had always encouraged me in anything I set out to do.

Father and son checking traps in the dark. Illustration by Sharon Davis

On arriving at our old homestead, Dad fired up the Coleman lantern and with a flashlight in hand we hiked in the pitch black dark up the secluded canyon. At eleven years old, I was quite aware that bears, cougars and other varmints were close at hand, but following Dad up the road made me a little bit braver than I otherwise would have been. We caught two beavers that night, the very first we had ever caught, but I remember much less about the beaver trapping than about what a great dad I had.

As Dad was checking one of our traps I moved upstream a few yards to check another trap, glancing suspiciously around in the dark and expecting a bear to appear momentarily. My small flashlight put out a feeble light as I stumbled to the trap and peered down into the dark water. Suddenly, just a few feet from me, it sounded as if a shot was fired as a large beaver slapped its tail on the water. This was the first time I ever heard a beaver slap its tail, and I must have jumped several feet.

It took me several hours to skin, flesh and stretch those first beaver pelts and each one had several holes in the not-so-valuable skin. Eventually I would learn to rough skin a beaver in less than three minutes but that would be many years and lots of holey beaver pelts down the river.

Big Game and Bear Hunting

When I was eleven years old I took the hunter's education class and in the fall of 1962 I hunted deer for the first time. Dad purchased an old 303 British rifle for me, cut the flared end of the barrel off with a hacksaw and worked the stock down to fit my small frame. He then filed a new front sight out of a silver dime and I was as happy as if I had a new custom rifle. That little gun served me well for several years and I eventually killed my first several bucks, my first bear and a bull elk with it before I moved up to an old Remington model 740, 30-06.

My first hunting trip with gun in hand was on the west side of Ward's Butte a little north of Curtin. This was the area where Dad and Uncle Howard had grown up. As usual I was with Dad hiking down an old logging road before full daylight on opening day of buck season. Our friends, the Blacks from Curtin, were with us and we all spread out in different directions for an early morning hunt.

Dad and I had gone just a short distance down an old logging road when he decided to stop and watch some small openings near some dense brush and wait for full daylight. He motioned for me to move about seventy-five feet above the road and watch one side of the same small opening. I could see for only about fifty feet and had barely climbed up on a small stump when the brush cracked in the direction I was watching. Within moments a nice three-point buck with its head low came sneaking out of the thicket and stood broadside no more than forty feet from me. Dad watched as I aimed as best I could due to the heavy gun and the buck fever that shook my entire body; after long seconds I pulled the trigger.

I fully expected the deer to drop in its tracks but it bolted with lightning speed and passed within a few feet of me while my jaw dropped. I forgot all about trying to shoot again and only watched as the buck leaped off the low bank thirty yards in front of Dad, to cross the narrow skid road. When the buck was in mid-air a shot rang out and the deer dropped stone dead in the middle of that little dirt road. Dad had taken him in the side of the head just under his eye. That wasn't the last time I saw dad shoot a deer in the head while it was running flat out. I suppose some luck was involved, but lots of practice and confidence always helps the luck. I didn't kill a deer that year but the next year I got my first deer by myself. It was just a small yearling buck, but just as memorable as any deer I ever harvested.

In 1964 I turned fourteen, and that September I killed my first bear while hunting in the Cascade Mountains near Spring Butte on upper Steamboat Creek. Up until that time I had hunted with Dad most of the time but had started sneaking off by myself when I got the chance. This area of the Calapooia Mountains, a sub-range of the Cascades, is very rugged with miles of old growth forests, rocky cliffs, rim rocks and some old clear cut logging areas. I drifted away from Dad and Mom and started dropping down a steep timbered ridge in a stand of old growth fir and hemlock timber. A quarter of a mile down into the canyon I startled something that crashed off

My First Bear! Illustration by Sharon Davis

down the hill. I followed on down the ridge a couple hundred yards, cautiously sneaking as I imagined my hero Daniel Boone would. I found a smoking fresh pile of bear scats but it never occurred to me that I had jumped a bear.

I stopped to light a match and watched the smoke drift down slope. Knowing that Daniel Boone would never hunt with the wind to his back I circled down the hill to a draw and headed uphill along a small trickle of a stream. Traveling slowly I accidentally stepped on a limb and it cracked under my foot. Stopping, I looked up the steep hill above me just as a big cinnamon-colored black bear stood up on its hind legs, paws draping in front, and swung its head from side to side searching for whatever had made the noise. It was the first bear I had ever seen.

As it dropped onto all fours, without hesitation I took aim behind its front shoulder and squeezed the trigger. I wasn't ready for what happened next as the bear let out a blood curdling roar and came straight down the hill, head over heels and directly at me. I turned tail and ran up the other side of the draw as fast as I could. I climbed up on a big windfall but all had become quiet and I couldn't see the bear.

Mom and Dad both heard the shot and all the bawling and roaring that the wounded bear was making. I could barely hear them yelling for me but I yelled back, "Dad, I wounded a grizzly!" Within a few minutes Dad came down into the canyon and we located the bear. It was quite dead, an adult female black bear of about 175 pounds. The .303 caliber bullet had gone right through the heart.

Little did I know at that time that bears would play a major role in my life. Eventually, I would personally capture a pile of bears and be responsible for taking many more over a thirty-year period doing damage control work for some of the largest timberland owners and managers, both public and private, in Oregon.

By late fall of 1964, I had hunted all season without scoring a buck. I was beginning to think that I was a pretty fair hunter by this time, having had three seasons of experience, but things were starting to look pretty gloomy and I was having second thoughts about my hunting skills. It was nearing the end of the buck season and Dad and I hurried out to Cedar Creek near Cottage Grove Lake for a quick hunt before dark. The rain was coming down as only it can in western Oregon. It was a bone-chilling, drenching rain with winds fresh off the Pacific Ocean.

I hunted up an old dirt skid road for a half an hour and then headed back toward the pickup to meet Dad. I was still a half mile from the truck and it was nearly dark as I shuffled along in the mud. Above the road some movement caught my eye about seventy-five feet up near a patch of vine maple. I could just barely make out two nice bucks feeding on the leaves.

With just enough backlight from the fading sky I quickly took aim behind the shoulder of the nearest buck and was momentarily blinded by the bright flash of the muzzle blast. As with the first buck I shot at, I expected this buck to drop in its tracks. Instead, it bolted at full speed with no apparent injury.

The buck quartered down and away from me toward the mud road where I was standing. As the buck jumped off the road bank only thirty yards from me, I fired. To my surprise, it dropped into the middle of the dirt, stone dead. The bullet had hit the nice three-point just under the eye. The first shot had taken the deer's heart out and it wouldn't have gone far, but I felt pretty good about the head shot.

I guess I inherited some of Dad's luck and confidence. It would take a few more years of experience before skill started to take the place of luck. It seems to me that nothing takes the place of dedicated hours in the field to create your own luck. Later that year, I downed my first bull elk in the Lookout Mountain area near Elgin. Nineteen-sixty-four turned out to be a pretty good year for the newest hunter in the Gilman family.

Bob Gilman displays well-handled furs in 1966.

Cliff and the Poachers

Cliff and I became good friends in high school. He was always laughing about everything and anything. He was also as mischievous as anyone could be. As he got older some would say he went way beyond mischievous but that's another story. Suffice to say that we had many good hunting, fishing and trapping trips, many of them during school hours. I can only count it as good luck that Cliff and I didn't end up in jail.

30

Cliff and I both loved to trap and each of us had several seasons of trapping experience by this time. Over Thanksgiving vacation of our junior year of high school we decided to go on a trapping adventure. Somehow I talked Dad into letting us use his four-wheel-drive pickup for several days. We gathered up Dad's entire elk hunting camp and headed over the mountain and down the Siuslaw River. We went only as far as Doe Creek, about fifteen miles below Lorane, and set up our wall tent and wood stove, cut fire wood and generally got camp all set.

After dinner that first evening we went out and killed a buck for camp meat and hung it up in the trees about a hundred yards from camp. The game warden checked us out a couple days later and it's a good thing he didn't come at supper time. He could have smelled that rutty buck cooking for a country mile. I couldn't eat a bite but Cliff loved it.

Cliff had had a few run-ins with this same game warden in the past couple of seasons and we were both a little on the nervous side as the warden asked to see our traps. Cliff's last run-in with the law came when his traps were not branded with the number issued from the Department of Fish and Wildlife. Every trapper has a lifetime number assigned when he or she first starts trapping and each trap is required to be marked with that number.

Being somewhat lax in the requirements of the law, Cliff hadn't bothered to follow through with this small detail since last season. I handed traps to the warden while Cliff searched through the pile looking for one with a brand on it. As I remember it was about one out of three traps that was actually branded, and Cliff would quickly put the unbranded ones down to look for one that was branded. All the while I would hand a trap to the warden and he would pretend to be looking it over very closely and inspect the brand. Cliff and I assumed we had really pulled the wool over this game warden's eyes, but looking back, it's for certain he was just letting us off easy.

Over the next few days we set traps in the Siuslaw and some of the local small creeks. We caught several beaver and one day we caught our first otter, a great thrill to us. The highlight of this trip, however, happened late on the last night.

Our tent was set up at an abandoned homestead site a short distance up Doe Creek. In those days the remains of homesteads were scattered for miles up and down the Siuslaw River valley. One main component of a homestead was an orchard, and the Doe Creek homestead had several old apple trees directly in front of our tent and between us and the gravel road. Our tent was not visible from the road due to a downhill slope behind the orchard that dropped the ground level by about fifteen feet.

We had just settled in for the night and turned off the gas lantern when several shots shattered the stillness. Let me tell you, when you are sixteen and someone shoots over the top of your tent you eject from your sleeping bag. Looking out the tent flap we saw light beams shining over the top of our tent and quickly realized that we weren't being shot at but that poachers were at work spotlighting deer in "our" apple orchard. Figuring this out was not too difficult for us since we were intimately familiar with spot lighting and poaching.

Cliff immediately had a plan for having some fun and wildly proclaimed that we should chase them! I protested momentarily but soon gave in and joined in his enthusiasm. Dad's pickup happened to be pointed directly toward the poacher vehicle. I fired up the engine and Cliff grabbed our big flashlight. I turned on the headlights and floored the pickup at the same time.

We came up over the embankment with all four wheels spinning and mud flying. Cliff had put a red stocking cap over the flashlight and began clicking it on and off. The poachers were parked about one hundred yards from where we came out to the road and they wasted no time in leaving the area. We, however, were not content with running them off but decided to continue the chase.

We had great fun and were laughing all the way until they outdistanced us four or five miles up the road and got away. I suppose those guys still think they outran the cops. We turned around and headed back to camp but stopped along the way to fill up our gas tank from some road equipment that the county crews had parked for the long weekend.

Another time Cliff and I decided to go to Waldo Lake on a fishing trip and Cliff's younger brother, Jack, came along with us. Jack would be killed in a car chase just a few short years later, trying to outrun the police. At the time of this story I believe Jack was about twelve years old and didn't yet know how to drive.

Cliff showed up with his old Willys Jeep and we loaded up our camping gear and were on our way. Cliff always had a big grin plastered on his face and he reminded me of the Alfred E. Newman character on the front of Mad magazine. This time his grin was broader than normal and I soon found out why. Cliff had "borrowed" a gallon of homemade wine from some old fellow who lived down the road from his place. Now keep in mind that Cliff and I didn't drink, at least to this point. We had just been too busy in the outdoors to have time for drinking. However, we were always opportunists and agreed that we should get drunk just to see what it was like.

I don't know for sure what was in that bottle but nothing in this world could have tasted any worse. It was some kind of wine but about a third of the gallon jug was filled with solid slimy lumps, not that we let that deter us. We started drinking it after we left Highway 58 where a Forest Service road leads toward Davis Lake. We let Jack drive since he was too young to drink, but it took him a day and a half to actually get us to Waldo Lake by the old Irish and Taylor Lake road.

Cliff and I didn't care for a couple of days: first, we were too drunk to care, then, because we were too sick to care. It took almost a week to recover from that drunk, and I didn't touch anything with alcohol in it for about fifteen years. I still rarely drink anything at all, but when I do it is in extremely moderate amounts and never homemade wine.

Romance, Marriage and the Dreadful Sawmill

About half way through my junior year of high school I met a beautiful young lady named Judy Bricker. I hadn't had much use for girls since Christy Bush had slapped me silly in the sixth grade but this was different. I was immediately smitten. Spending time with her even started to cut into some of my hunting and fishing time. Cliff was so disgusted with me that he went and found some new friends. Looking back, that wasn't such a bad thing since Cliff and I had definitely been headed for trouble with the law. I think Cliff may have proven that a little later and he disappeared to Canada for a few years. On the other hand, Judy Bricker started me down the road of the straight and narrow. It took me a while but I eventually learned to keep my wheels between the two track ruts.

Judy and I went together through high school and were married August 31, 1968. We soon had two children. Kelly was born in December of 1969, and Sam in March of 1972. I continued my outdoor pursuits but they were somewhat limited after I started working for Judy's Uncle Frank at R&R Cedar Mill in Cottage Grove.

Our first house was a rental house out on South Sixth Street near the old drive-in theater. The house was pretty miserable and full of mice, which gave me full opportunity to show my new bride what a skilled trapper she had married. The winter of 1968 brought one of the heaviest snowfalls in Oregon history. The snow fell three feet deep in the lowlands around Cottage Grove with higher amounts in the surrounding hills. This snowfall temporarily put me out of my

Robert and Judy Gilman at the Sweethearts Banquet in the early years of marriage.

part-time trapping business, but I continued to work at R&R. Everyone else was laid off for about two weeks, but I was the night watch at the mill and shoveled snow off uncovered work areas to help get R&R back to work.

At R&R I started out doing cleanup work under the planer chain and soon graduated to feeding the hog, a big grinder used to shred much of the waste material from the mill into a usable fuel byproduct. I was no stranger to hard work, although before this I had mostly worked for myself. I worked hard for Uncle Frank and he rewarded me by allowing me to try new jobs around the mill. Within a couple of years I had mastered most of the jobs outside the mill and could run most of the equipment. During my years at the sawmill I continued to trap for furs on a limited scale. We were working most of the time, six days a week, nine hours a day, but I managed to trap after work, over holidays, and when we would occasionally be out of work. In the mid-1970s fur prices were starting to rise a little and the extra money always came in handy with a wife and two small children.

In my third year at R&R, our long-time trimmer man in the mill quit and Frank needed a replacement. At the time, I thought I could handle anything and asked for the chance to try out for the job. Uncle Frank wasn't very enthusiastic, but since he didn't have anyone else who could handle this difficult job he gave me a try.

I ended up spending the next three years on that gang trimmer and they were among the most difficult days of my life. The Oxbow fire had burned a few years before and almost all the cedar we were cutting was out of the burn. The first log to hit the head rig at 7:00 a.m. each day would fog the mill with fine cedar dust, so that many times you couldn't see from one end of the mill to the other, a distance of about one hundred feet. The dust wouldn't clear until the saws were shut down at lunch and again a 5:00 p.m.

The gang trimmer was an old trip-lever model with numerous levers, buttons, foot pedals and conveyer chains. The trim saws consisted of twelve twenty-four-inch saws spaced two feet apart that could be manually tripped to cut lumber to various lengths or pieces. I often had lumber piled and tangled four feet deep for hours at a time as I struggled to trim each board to various lengths and grades.

On two different occasions while doing this job, I came close to being run through the saws. Both times a board came up the incline chains and on to the deck that fed into the trim saws and was sticking out beyond where I was standing. The boards would drop off the incline chains and onto lugged chains that automatically fed the boards into the trim saws. These feed chains were controlled by a foot pedal. A switch on the wall on my right side could also kill the feeder chains into the saws.

Twice I didn't notice soon enough that the boards were sticking out and they hit me in the side, knocking me off balance. The lugs on the chains caught the boards and automatically pushed me back-wards into the trimmer. One time I was able to stop the chains with the foot petal but it was a very close call. The other time I was too late to reach the foot petal and the board already had me bent over forwards, pushing me through the two-foot-high opening into the trim saw and conveyer chains. At the very last moment I was able to reach my right arm behind my back and up over my head to switch off the automatic conveyer chains. It just could not have been any closer without breaking me into small pieces, but I pulled the lumber up to its proper position on the chains, fired up the gang trimmer and went back to work.

You might assume that this sort of event would scare you to death, but the fact is it happens so quickly that it is over before you can get excited. It is only in hindsight that the reality of the situation becomes clear. As I have learned several times over the years, it is a short distance between life and death.

During this time I learned that some men in sawmills are not happy people and seem to enjoy spreading their unhappiness around. I also learned I was too young and inexperienced to handle the re-sponsibility and stress of this difficult job. At 145 pounds I didn't have the strength to handle some of the "cants" that weighed as much as three times my weight, the cedar dust made me sick every day, and I dreamed, or rather had nightmares, about work almost every night.

I might have been able to overcome those obstacles but the edger man had decided that he didn't like me. By the way he ran the edger he could cause me trouble and he used every opportunity he had to bury me in tangled lumber. He never once did it when the boss was around, but once I was covered up it would take hours of furious work to catch up.

After almost three years of this constant battle, I broke down bawling as I left the mill one day and I knew it was time to quit. I didn't know how I would feed my family or pay the bills but I vowed never to return to that sawmill. I later broke that vow for a few months but I knew it was temporary and I have never regretted putting sawmills in my past.

Winter was near and the price of furs was climbing, so I quickly decided that I would trap for a living. I didn't know it at the time, but that disastrous ending to six years in the sawmill put me on the road to a full-time trapping business. The year was 1975 and I have trapped every winter since that time. My trapping eventually turned into a regular business that not only provided for my family, but employed numerous other trappers over the years.

My son, Sam, followed me into the business and became one of my top bear and mountain beaver (boomer) trappers. Later on, Sam and I together started Ketch-Um Wildlife Control. A business to assist people with preventing wildlife damage and capture problem wildlife in urban and suburban areas. Sam eventually took over most field work for Ketch-Um Wildlife Control, turned it into a full-time job and became a master at solving all sorts of urban wildlife/human conflicts.

My first winter of full-time trapping wasn't too bad. I made enough money to pay most of the bills and put food on the table. It wasn't a lot different than working in the mill, except it was a lot more fun. Either way, there never seemed to be enough money to go around. After the season, I was well satisfied and deemed it the most enjoyable winter of work since I had been married.

After trapping season was over I had to get a job quickly. Uncle Frank tried to get me to come back to work for him but I just couldn't face going back to the sawmill. I continued to have a good relationship with Frank but I knew it was time for a major change. Working in the woods paid good money in those days, and after a little thought I decided to try to find work setting chokers for a logging outfit.

Our longtime friends, the Blacks from Curtin, were a logging family of several brothers, all with their own businesses. Some had trucks, others had Cats, and the oldest brother, Lloyd, had a high-lead logging outfit. I applied for a job, and after warning me of the dangers and how hard I would have to work, Lloyd hired me. Dad really tried hard to talk me out of going to work in the woods. He had been a logger for many years early in life and knew how dangerous it was. As usual, I listened, but with a family to feed and with some stubbornness I made my choice and went ahead.

I worked almost a year for the Black Brothers logging outfit. We logged up Big River above Cottage Grove Lake in huge old growth timber. Gary Black was the lead choker setter and Bill Black was the rigging slinger. They were both my age and we had grown up together hunting, fishing and occasionally trapping together. Gary's mom and dad, Mutt and Clara Black, were my folks' best friends for years and we had often camped together. We had a great time setting chokers and talking all day, every workday, about hunting, fishing and trapping.

Setting chokers was easy most of the time, but moving roads was a different story. A road is a strip of hillside where a main cable runs through a block (pulley) that is strapped to a large stump. When the line goes through the block and back up to the yarder it's called the "haul back." Chokers are hooked to the mainline by the rigging and reach out about thirty feet in each direction from the mainline. This makes a road about seventy feet wide down the hill.

When all the logs are pulled up to the landing from top to bottom of the hill, a new road has to be made. This requires several steps.

All of the cables have to be dropped to the ground and the tail block is moved around the hill to start a new road. A smaller cable called a "haywire" is pulled by hand through the new block so that all the big cables can be rethreaded through the tail block. Pulling the haywire is an easy process. You just pull cable until your arms are ready to fall off and then continue to pull until the job is done, however long that takes. If you can't do that, the boss will find someone who can and you can catch the next truck back to town.

With the big log yarder that Lloyd had set up, we were using a sixteen-inch tail block, no small piece of steel. I think it weighed about 125 pounds and had to be moved by hand. The choker setters always took turns moving the tail block. The first time it was my turn I decided it would be easiest to drag the thing instead of packing it. I was pretty certain that at 145 pounds, I couldn't pack it anyway.

After dragging that block for about two hundred feet over logs, stumps, brush and rocks I thought I would die from exhaustion. No one gave me any advice or help. Loggers don't need to do that; you either make it, or you don't. The next time it was my turn I hoisted the block up on my shoulder and carried it to the new tail hold. Carrying the block turned out to be much easier than dragging it through the brush.

One Friday evening just before quitting time, it was Bill Black's turn to carry the tail block. We were changing roads at the end of the day so we would be all set up on Monday morning. We were working in a big canyon in the Calapooia Range and the tree cut line was about halfway down the hill. The yarder was probably four hundred yards above us and the canyon bottom about that far below us down a very steep mountain.

Bill carried the block over to the new tail hold and dropped it on the ground. The block started rolling and rolled all the way to the bottom of the canyon. It seemed like we could hear it crashing for three minutes before it came to rest in the tangled bottom.

Needless to say we went down and packed it out, three of us taking turns, and no one complained. After that we were all very careful how we dropped the block when moving roads.

Much of the winter we were snowed out of work, and I again spent a good deal of time trapping furs to make enough money to feed my family. I worked for less than a year in the woods and much of that time we were out of work. With low humidity during summer and the consequent fire danger and deep winter snow that continually put us out of work, it was clear that this was a tough way to make a living. It was also clear to me that I wasn't as tough as any logger that I ever met. Trapping was looking better all the time and fur prices continued to climb.

The Art of Tracking

In 1976, Judy and I bought our first house. It was an old 1914 two-story house on about an acre of ground and just inside the city limits of Cottage Grove. The house needed a lot of work, but by this time I had worked for several summers doing carpenter work for Judy's dad, Glen. I was always independent and would quit each winter to go trapping. I'm sure this drove my father-in-law crazy as he probably figured I should continue to work on a steady job instead of wasting each winter trapping. I started remodeling the old house and had it fairly comfortable by early winter of 1976.

When trapping season opened I started stringing traps, primarily for beaver, but I also had a good number of bobcat traps set out. Cats had until recently been worth only a few dollars, but suddenly the price rose to twenty-five to thirty dollars apiece for Coast Range bobcats. That was more than beaver were worth at the time, so I started spending about equal time on bobcats and beaver.

The beaver season at that time ended on February 15 each year, but bobcats were considered predators and there was no season closure or limits. Bobcat pelts stayed in good condition until April, so I continued trapping those predators until mid-April each spring for several years, until they were reclassified as a furbearer with a February 15 closing date.

I had been catching bobcats since 1972 when I worked at R&R Cedar Mill and trapped nights and weekends. I took my first bobcat when I hiked into Hawley Creek just east of Lorane over on the headwaters of the Siuslaw where I was trapping beaver. When something started eating one of the beaver carcasses, I set a No. 1 ½ longspring trap and soon caught my first bobcat. By 1976, I was catching twenty-five to thirty per season and felt myself fairly proficient in cat trapping. In those years both beaver and bobcats were very numerous in the cut-over forest lands in the Coast Range of Oregon.

Hawley Creek had been logged in the 1950s and the stream was choked with beaver ponds by 1976. It was too far off the road to pack beaver out so I started skinning them on the spot. The bottom of this canyon was a spooky place after dark and that helped in my speed skinning lessons. I eventually got pretty fast and once skinned a beaver at a fur sale contest at Salem in just over two and a half minutes. I also finally got to where I could flesh, stretch and nail out a blanket beaver pelt in about sixteen to eighteen minutes. It took me years of hard work and several hundred beaver pelts to get up to that speed.

Like most other skills that I developed over the years, I got my inspiration from someone else. In about 1963, I read an article in *Fur Fish & Game* magazine by Ray Black, a Canadian trapper. He had won the 1962 skinning contest at the Ontario Trappers Association Annual Convention in North Bay, Ontario, by skinning and stretching a medium beaver in just over twenty minutes. At the time I read that article, it was taking me close to two hours to put up a beaver pelt and it usually had several holes cut in it. With instructions and inspiration from Ray Black, along with many years of experience, I finally achieved a similar level of expertise.

One year while trapping the Siuslaw, I floated my canoe into my trapping camp and threw nine beavers out on the river bank to go with the ten I had captured the day before. I decided to make a game out of skinning these beaver and see how fast I could get the job done.

I laid out my axe and steel, sharpened my butcher knife and a straight-bladed slitting knife. I then got a good piece of stove wood to chop on and piled all the beaver close by. I checked my watch, and at 3:00 p.m. I grabbed a beaver and went to work. I took each one of 19 beavers, and with my two-and-a-half-pound camper's axe I cut off the feet and tails. I then did a similar process by making the center slit from tail to chin on each beaver.

After the initial preparation, I picked one of the four smaller size beavers to do first, since they always seem more difficult to me. After the small beavers were rough-skinned, I started in on the remaining 15 beaver using my steel a couple of times, while skinning each animal and using the straight knife to skin around the head. When all 19 beaver were pelted I looked at my watch and it was 4:03 p.m.. This was the fastest that I ever rough-skinned a big pile of beavers. I attribute that level of speed to a trapper I had never met, but who inspired me through his articles to continually strive to be faster and more skilled at skinning.

One trapping adventure on Hawley Creek was especially memorable. I had hiked into the canyon one weekend, set up several beaver and bobcat traps, and then checked the traps after work during the week. By hurrying up the mountain after work and hiking quickly down into the canyon, I could start checking traps by dark, skin anything I caught and start the long steep climb back to my truck. It was usually about two and a half hours from the time I started checking traps in the dark until I had climbed out to the truck.

It was a Friday evening in late November, and a heavy pounding rain was bursting from the nearly black clouds as I departed my truck and started down the old skid trails that snaked down the mountain for half a mile before intersecting Hawley Creek. The strong southwest winds were blowing as they often do in western Oregon when the Pineapple Express brings the moisture filled clouds off the Pacific Ocean and into this part of the Coast Range mountains.

As I hiked down the mountain on the old muddy skid trail, I noticed two sets of large dog tracks had followed me out of the canyon on my last trip to check the traps. This was a little unsettling since it was a long ways to the nearest house, and I had seen no dog tracks on the roads leading into this canyon on several other trips.

I continued down into the dark gloomy canyon, and I began to remember all the stories I had read about the packs of wild dogs in the eastern United States. A little feeling of fear traveled up through my stomach and into my chest, but I knew the traps had to be checked tonight no matter how dark and gloomy this place had become. I had the next three days off and needed to pull this little trapline. I planned to pull this line and put out a new line farther down the Siuslaw starting tomorrow morning.

Just before I came to the end of the old cat road, I saw the unmistakable fresh prints of two large dogs in the mud. They had been traveling up the trail toward me and had turned around heading back in the direction that I was going. It wasn't difficult to tell the tracks were smoking fresh in this pouring down rain storm. The hair on the back of my neck bristled as I pulled my big flashlight out and shined it down into the jumbled brushy creek bottom and old beaver ponds. Nothing moved, and I comforted myself by placing my hand on the butt of my well-worn Ruger Single Six pistol that always traveled with me on my traplines.

I had a dozen traps set along the beaver ponds that were spread out over about a half mile of the creek below me. Half of them were No. 3 longsprings set for bobcats, and the other six were No. 14 Oneida jump traps set for beaver. The beaver traps were rigged on a slide wire system with sacks of rocks for weights to quickly drown any beavers that were captured. I hadn't expected to catch much on this trip since this line had been out for a while, and recently I had shortened it in preparation for pulling out of this drainage. Numerous critters had already been harvested and it was time to move on. My plan was to quickly grab those dozen traps, throw them into my little Hawbakers' pack basket, and beat feet for the top of the mountain and the warm dry security of my truck.

As always, the weather played a critical role in my catch, good or bad, and it was soon evident that the low pressure and big storm coming in had caused a big movement of animals preceding the storm that was now striking in full force. The first three beaver traps yielded a blanket and an extra-large beaver, and a big tom bobcat was in the first cat trap. Toward the end of the line, I caught another blanket beaver and another medium-sized tom bobcat. This was a lot of fur for a short trapline that I had thought was used up, and now I had a big load to pack out of this dark canyon.

I had pulled the traps and left the critters lay on the way down the creek since the line had to be backtracked to return to the truck. The earlier fear I had felt was somewhat diminished as I kept busy checking and pulling traps, and it felt good to bang off a couple of rounds from the single six to dispatch the bobcats. The crack of the pistol had momentarily made me feel like it would scare the shadowy fanged critters that might be lurking just out of sight in the dark wet brush. I pulled out my skinning knife and as quickly as possible ripped the skin off the beaver, and five minutes later dropped it into the bottom of the pack basket.

As I was skinning the beaver, my sight pattern dropped to the small area in front of me where I was skinning. By necessity the flashlight was placed on a chunk of wood and could no longer be used to scan the immediate area around me until I had finished with the beaver.

While concentrating on peeling the beaver, I suddenly felt chills go up my back, and the hair on my neck bristled again. It was raining hard, the wind was blowing, and it was pitch black outside the small ring of light my flashlight was making. I grabbed the flashlight and scanned a circle behind me, then a circle all around. No eyes showed up, but the brush surrounded me tightly and twenty-five feet was about the maximum range of my light. It felt much better to get my hand back on the light, and I dropped the pelt into the basket along with some traps and started back up the creek bottom, gathering traps and fur as I went.

The bobcats were brought out whole, but each of the beavers was skinned in turn. Each time I laid down the flashlight, I had the same feeling of something close-by watching me. The fear would take hold, but then diminish as I got control of the light and was able to scan the area around me. Looking back, I suppose it was just my imagination working overtime, but I must say I have spent many hours in dark lonely places checking traps, and that hair-raising feeling has only made its appearance on one other occasion.

The other time that my sixth sense kicked in was many years later. I was checking bear snares and checked the last one right at dusk. I ran up off the road to the snare and found that a big bear had come in to the back side of a crib and stole the beef head I was using for bait. The bear had taken the head a few feet away, laid down and made a perfect imprint where he had wrapped his front paw around the head, and used a claw of his other paw to neatly slit the skin on top of the skull as if cut by a knife. It was obvious I had scared the bear off when he was getting ready for his evening meal.

I gathered up the beef head, rewired it to the back of my cubby and was in the process of blocking off access to the back of the crib, when all the hair on the back of my neck bristled, and all of my senses suddenly became wide awake. Hearing, sight and smell had all become extremely acute from one moment to the next. I knew instantly that the bear had circled and was watching me, but try as I might, I couldn't spot him in the thick brush.

I slowly backed out of the brushy little draw, went back to my truck and left the area. I never had a second thought about staying to finish my work; my sixth sense had kicked in and worked perfectly, and I didn't see any sense in ignoring the warning.

Many years spent mostly alone in the outdoors has convinced me that we all have a sixth sense. It is probably deeply suppressed in most of us but can quickly appear in some circumstances. The most amazing thing to me is how all your senses can instantly focus on the subject at hand when it kicks in. While a sixth sense may be deeply suppressed, the feeling of fear, at least with me, seems to be just barely under the skin. It can appear at a moment's notice without much prodding.

Looking back over many years, I can say that a little fear is a good thing. It has given me caution when entering into rapids on a river, slowed me down while crossing a slippery log over a high ravine and generally helped me to be prepared before something bad happens. I don't much like discomfort or pain and a little fear has helped me to avoid both of them on numerous occasions.

Back on Hawley Creek at the upper end of the beaver dams I loaded the last of the three rough-skinned beaver pelts into my little pack basket. The dozen traps and three beaver pelts had packed it clear to the top rim and it was a heavy load. I swung the canvas straps over my shoulders and hoisted the basket up on my back. It felt like it was full of lead as I staggered to my feet and then balanced the two cats over the top and hung on to the feet to keep them in place.

From the top end of the beaver dams it was another quarter mile up the creek to where the old skid road headed up the mountain and about three quarters of a mile to the truck. The rain and wind had finally let up some and the torment of packing the heavy load up a difficult trail induced me to think only about where I would put my feet. The big white fangs of my recent imagination faded away as I labored up the trail, but every once in a while the feeling of fear would lighten my load and push me along at a little faster pace.

About halfway up the mountain I realized that there was a big switchback in the skid road and a short cut straight up the hill would cut my hike by about one half. The quicker I could get out of this dark canyon the better, so I turned and started clawing my way up the steep brushy mountain.

Part-way up the cow's face one of my canvas pack basket straps suddenly snapped, putting the entire weight of the load on one shoulder. Even though the steep mountainside with dense brush, blackberry vines and numerous downed small logs and limbs was a nightmare to climb through, the several-year-old clear-cut was still a friendlier place than the bottom of that dark canyon. The dense second growth fir and cedar stands that crowded the creek bottom up next to the brushy beaver dams along the creek made Hawley Creek a scary place that night, and I was very happy to leave it behind me.

Somehow I was able to struggle up that steep brushy hill with one hand holding the flashlight and the other balancing two bobcats on top of my full pack basket with the broken strap. Under normal circumstances, I don't think I could have climbed that hill with all that awkward weight, but the winds of fear and adrenalin just seemed to push me right up that dark rainy mountain.

It was a good feeling to see my truck in the flashlight beam and throw that heavy load in the back. I headed home, skinned the bobcats and hung up the furs to dry a little before I would put them in the freezer. The next morning I was up early and headed back up over the mountain to the headwaters of the Siuslaw. I was headed for Dogwood Creek where I had spotted a number of beaver dams earlier in the fall.

The Dog Man and the Trapper

In January 1978, I was checking traps on Dogwood Creek a few miles downriver from Siuslaw Falls when a young guy about my age pulled up with a pickup full of hound dogs and introduced himself as Dewey Walton.

At that time many hound hunters and trappers weren't getting along too well. In fact the rivalry and competition for cat pelts would soon cause many small wars to break out between these two groups. However, Dewey and I hit it off and eventually became good friends. We spent an hour discussing trapping and hunting and I soon found out that Dewey was also a carpenter who had worked in the trade since high school. Dewey was one of the best dog hunters and trainers around and knew bobcats, bears and cougar from A to Z. Since we both had the same desire to hunt and trap as much as possible, we soon formed a partnership and decided to go into business for ourselves building houses and doing remodel work during the summer. This would leave us free to hunt and trap from late fall to late winter each year.

The house that Judy and I purchased on R Street in Cottage Grove was on a large corner lot, and I soon discovered that it could be subdivided into three lots. I had the place surveyed and subdivided and then somehow talked the First National Bank loan officer into loaning me enough money to build a spec house on one of the lots. We were pretty much penniless and in debt at the time, and I'm sure it didn't hurt that my mother worked at the bank when I secured that loan.

In the spring of 1978, Dewey and I started work on our first new house together. We did almost all the work ourselves and subcontracted as little as possible. We finished up the job in early fall and sold the house right away. We then put away our carpenter tools and started hunting and trapping. This was a pattern we kept up each year until I went to work for the U.S. Fish and Wildlife Service in 1986 on a spring bear trapping job for some timber companies.

Dewey taught me some things about cat behavior, and I showed him what I knew at the time about trapping bobcats. Over the next few years we spent many happy hunting and camping trips, together. Dewey always had his hounds with him on these trips and we chased cougar, bear and bobcats just for the fun of it in summer and fall. Dewey would then hunt with his dogs and trap all winter, and I would trap.

Dewey and I would talk trapping all spring and summer making big plans for fall and winter. One summer we decided to rig all our cat traps up with six feet of trap chain and steel hook drags. Dewey contacted a steel supplier in Eugene and had several hundred one-half-inch rebar steel drags bent to shape. We then bought hundred-foot rolls of trap chain and rigged all our predator traps with these drags. Up until that time, I had used wire to tie off all my traps to a nearby tree. This new setup made setting a trap very fast and they could be set almost anywhere without need for something to tie off to. Bobcats would usually get tangled up in the brush within a few feet of where the trap was set. Coyotes and cougars were a different story and would sometimes go half a mile with our poorly designed trap drags.

Over the next several years I trailed dozens of bobcats, coyotes and a few cougars that were captured in traps using these drags. Trailing the drag mark of a half-pound rebar after it has rained hard for forty-eight to seventy-two hours taught me the finer points of tracking. Bobcats had reached prices of eighty to one hundred dollars for Coast Range cats and sometimes exceeded two hundred and

Trapping friends and partners (from left) Dave Vann, Dewey Walton, Ivan Gagner and Jerry Eckstine at the Waldo Lake Trappers Rendezvous about 1980.

fifty dollars for High Cascade type cats. This was big money and encouraged me to excel in the art of tracking when one of my traps would be missing from where it had been set.

Dewey showed me a number of tracking tricks that he had learned in his years of trailing hounds. Several years later, I would surprise professional foresters by identifying a bobcat track from one partial toe print, spotting cougar tracks on a gravel road in the early morning dew, or spotting a bear track coming off a dirt bank while we were doing thirty miles an hour in a truck. One thing that these foresters didn't know was that I knew where the bear would cross the road before we got there. Bears and other animals have the habit of crossing roads in the same areas time after time.

Years of experience had taught me where these crossings were located. Of course these are common practices for experienced trappers and dog hunters. The art of tracking is not only the observation of tracks, but, as one author put it, it is the "art of seeing."

Animals leave a variety of evidence of their passing, and sometimes those signs can be identified for many years after passing through. Bears, for instance, can leave numerous different kinds of signs or evidence of their passing. Bite trees or marking posts can be identified for many years after being marked or can be identified as being freshly marked. Bear hair can often be seen on rubbing posts and very often USFS sign post are used by bear to mark territory boundaries.

Various sizes of bear tracks can help identify the size and sex of the animal. Obscure tracks and trails made in tall grass can

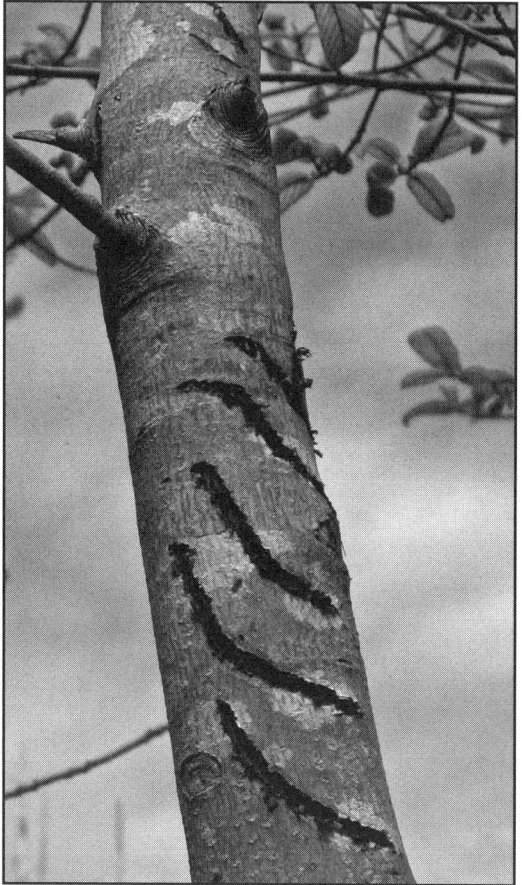

A cascara tree marked by a bear will show its marks for many years.

quickly identify fresh bear activity by the skilled tracker while remaining invisible or incomprehensible to most people. A tree with the bark peeled off could be a porcupine, pack rat, squirrel, snowshoe hare, mountain beaver, river beaver, elk or a bear. A seasoned tracker can tell very quickly based on tooth marks, type of tree, size and location of peeling, and even the time of year, which animal has recently or many years in the past traveled the path that led by a tree or other sign.

In addition to trapping I often used my tracking experience while hunting for deer and elk. Over the years I have tracked and taken numerous deer and elk by this hunting method. Snow tracking is often easily accomplished if snow conditions are right, as compared with tracking on dry ground.

Many hunters enjoy tracking elk in snow. If you don't believe that you should try to find a fresh elk track in the general hunting season on public land that doesn't have a human track behind it! I suspect very few of these trackers ever catch up with the elk they are trailing. If you are not willing to stay with them for several miles and make a complete physical and mental commitment, then you might as well not start on the track of an elk or a mule deer buck for that matter.

One year while hunting for mule deer in the Fort Rock area of central Oregon, I tracked a fine buck in the dry sand of the desert sage brush. This buck was the exception to the rule and I only tracked it for half a mile before making the kill. It wasn't often that I killed a buck the first time I jumped him, but in this case a quartering away running shot at 456 paces downed my buck. Sometimes you need a little luck, but I have found that you can't track down a buck if you don't stick with the track, and you can't kill him without shooting.

On another occasion while hunting elk in the Chemult area, I tracked a five-point bull for seven hours across dry ground, pine forest and lodge pole pine thickets before I killed him. This elk hunt was without question the most memorable hunt of my life, and I will tell that story a little later in this book. Tracking conditions were perfect for this hunt, and they are always a key factor in success or failure while tracking big game.

Highly-refined tracking skills are lost to most of today's hunters. Some of the old-time hunters had skills that most hunters of today can only dream about. I am one of those hunters who dreamed of acquiring those skills and have spent a fair amount of time in pursuit

Seven hours of dry ground tracking brought down this bull in the Chemult area before the snow arrived.

of that mostly lost art.

Van Houston was one of those old-timers who developed hunting skills that are almost unheard of today. At one time Van Houston was probably the best known coyote trapper in eastern Oregon. My friend, Rick Farthing, hunted and trapped with Van when Rick was a young man, and Van passed on many of his trapping and hunting skills to Rick.

Van's passions in life seemed to be trapping coyotes and tracking big buck deer. He tracked and killed some monster bucks over the years, and when it came to coyotes he had a personal best of thirty coyotes on one check of his trapline! He obviously did an excellent job educating Rick, and I believe that Rick is one of the most-accomplished hunters that I have ever known.

It was Rick who first told me about Van's tracking skills and shared a few tidbits of methods Van had learned and passed on to

Rick in a lifetime of tracking big bucks. My friendship with Rick and knowing a little of the legendary tracking skills of Van Houston was what first inspired my desire to start tracking bucks and bulls. The first buck I tracked in the high desert sage near Fort Rock was a direct result of Rick's stories about Van Houston and his great tracking ability.

Van had grown up near a stage stop named Fife in the southeast corner of Crook County Oregon. He was born March 20, 1905, and lived out most of his life in the general area near Prineville. Fife was not too far from the current G.I. Ranch north of Highway 20 and east of Brothers. In his younger years, Van had herded sheep and been a buckaroo in the Oregon High Desert for the well-known rancher Bill Brown.

One year, Van was camped out at the old long-gone community of Fife and was getting ready to do some coyote trapping as soon as the buck deer season was over. Van was in camp when a hunter came by and stopped to talk. In the discussion Van learned this guy was one of a party of five hunters. They were doctors and lawyers from out of the area and it seemed they were more interested in partying than hunting. The fellow informed Van that they had hunted all over the area and were sure that there weren't many deer, let alone bucks, in this area. So far they had seen only one small buck.

Van was a lifelong resident hunter/trapper of this area and knew better. This was good big buck country and Van knew where those bucks were hiding. He made a deal with this guy and his four companions and told them that the next day he would show them some big bucks. A few days later the professionals had filled all their tags with big mature desert mule bucks.

The story didn't make clear to me who actually shot those bucks, and I'm not sure if anyone alive today knows for sure, but it was without a doubt Van Houston who tracked each one of them down. When Van got on a track, it was always a big buck. He used a wooden match

Van Houstan's 9 by 11 by 39-inch non-typical mule deer buck draped over the fender of his 1936 Chevrolet in the late 1930s.

stick to measure the heal width of the track, and if the track wasn't as wide as the match was long, he wouldn't take the track.

One of Van's biggest bucks was a nontypical nine-by-eleven mule deer with a thirty-nine-inch spread that he tracked down in the late 1930s. Van's brother, Sumner, was crossing a plowed field on the Salt Creek Ranch near Roberts when he spotted a monster buck track. Sumner contacted Van in Prineville, and later that day Van took up the track with intentions of filling his buck tag.

Since it was late in the day, Van took a light bed roll on his back and set out at a fast pace. Knowing well the habits of these big bucks, Van took his boots off and slowed to a snail's pace when he approached the area where he thought the buck would bed down for the day. In this case as often happens, the buck caught sight or smell of Van, jumped and was gone despite Van's caution and skill, before he could get a shot off. One quick look told Van this was the giant buck of a lifetime.

Van dogged the track all afternoon but the buck was uncommonly cagey and continued to evade the hunter. At dark Van stopped under a convenient juniper tree and spent the night wrapped in his blanket. The next morning at daylight he again took up the track and soon found where the buck had started to wander and feed. It was a slow confusing process to sort out the track but eventually Van lined out on the buck and tracked him to his bed where he was again jumped with only a quick sighting.

This cat and mouse game went on most of the day as Van momentarily sighted the buck on several occasions. As the day progressed the buck allowed Van to get closer and closer, whether out of curiosity about the man following him or letting his caution be lulled away because nothing bad had happened. Van was slowly closing in.

It is not at all uncommon for a buck to go three to five miles or farther from a good feeding area to a secure bedding ground. Van had tracked this buck to his first bedding area and then followed him most of the next day. Van told Rick that after several miles on the second day the buck was approaching the main highway which was probably the main Bear Creek Road. Van was aware of the caution the buck would use when crossing this road and he again removed his shoes and moved slowly, frequently stopping to scan ahead.

With the eye of the experienced hunter Van finally spotted the old silver grey muzzle of the buck he was tracking. No other part of the deer could be seen in among thick junipers, save a small bit of brown antler and that dead giveaway of the old grey/white muzzle. With one of his favorite guns, a weathered, buckhorn-sighted 32/20 Winchester, Van put the bead on the brush a few inches behind the clearly visible muzzle and pulled the trigger. The monster buck dropped in his tracks, with one shot just under the eye.

Van had the horns of this beautiful buck mounted and it hung in his Prineville home for many years until the house burned down in 1978. The picture of that magnificent buck draped across the hood of his 1936 Chevrolet is all that remains.

There is a lot more to the story of this extraordinary outdoorsman

Van Houston (left) and a trailer full of big bucks.

and it is too bad someone didn't get more of his adventures down in print. I heard this story directly from Rick Farthing, who trapped coyotes with Van in the 1970s. Rick had the picture of Van with that trailer load of big bucks hanging in his taxidermy shop, and each time I looked at it I was in awe of the skills needed to accomplish such a feat.

I never developed skills in tracking bucks that would in any way compare with Van Houston or many other old-time hunters, but tracking bucks and bulls has remained one of the greatest and most enjoyable challenges for me of all the outdoor activities that I have ever pursued. Each time I take a track of a nice buck, I am reminded of Van posing with that impressive pile of trophy bucks.

When on a big track I am also reminded that there is much more to it than just following the hoof prints to the end of the trail. You need to know when to go fast and when to go in your stocking feet at a snail's pace. Frankly, I have learned over and over that I should have been going slower. Tracking doesn't do much good if you don't eventually spot the buck or bull before he spots you. This is an area in which I can claim great expertise. In my many years of tracking bucks and bulls, I have "not seeing him before he sees me" down to an art form.

On the other hand, if you can't cover a lot of ground when the elk are traveling fast, you may never catch them. Their tracks, pace and actions will tell you when to move fast or slow. As I pointed out earlier, tracking is "the art of seeing," but once you have observed the sign you need to determine what it means.

When a bull first starts to fishhook or circle, he may be getting ready to bed down, but chances are he is watching his back trail and getting downwind to see if anything is following him. The wind direction may be an insignificant thing to us dull-nosed humans, but bucks and bulls live and die by the slightest puff of a breeze. Sometimes these critters don't believe their eyes and ears, but when it comes to smell, they know their enemies and always react instantly.

The bucks, bulls and even cows usually win when I am tracking, but I never get discouraged. Tracking is in my blood, and even though I will never excel to the level of many of the old-timers, I love the tracking challenge almost as much as trapping. *Rick Farthing's excellent tracking skills led to this encounter with a good buck.*

59

Cat Skull Camp on Leopold Creek, a tributary of Esmond Creek in the Siuslaw drainage. Illustration by Sharon Davis

Cat Skull Camp

From the early 1970s until the mid-1980s, I set up and ran long traplines for beaver, bobcats, otter and other furbearers. Fur prices had been rising and my entire winter income now depended on furs. At different times my trapline areas included selected areas of eastern Oregon, the Willamette Valley, and the Cascade and Coast Range mountains. One of my favorite areas during this time was the Siuslaw drainage in the Coast Range. My usual trapline on this drainage would start about five miles below Lorane and extend as far as the west side of Roman Nose Mountain. I would often have a trapline laid out over a 150-mile circuit. Over the years I used several different camps while running this line. My usual plan would be to camp out and trap for five to six days at a time, then return home to freeze my furs, re-supply and quickly return for more trapping.

For several different years starting in 1975, I set up my tent camp on Leopold Creek where it runs into Esmond Creek, just up from its confluence with the Siuslaw River. The first year, I camped on the north side of Leopold Creek in a superb stand of old growth timber. The Douglas fir in this stand were enormous in size, many six feet or more in diameter and well over two hundred feet tall.

This was a great camping spot with a beautiful clear mountain stream only a few feet from my tent door, with excellent populations of beaver, otter and bobcats close by. I set up my wall tent, cut plenty of firewood and had a very comfortable trapping camp. The only small problem was the dirt road that ran off the gravel logging road back into my tent site. It had a tendency to turn to mud as the torrential winter rains progressed.

In late January of that year, my good friend Gary Black decided to come down to my camp and spend a few days running traps with me. We had often hunted, fished and camped together, and I enjoyed having some company on occasion. The previous year, I had skinned several bobcats near where my tent was now set up, and one day Gary spotted those skulls in the brush. In short order, we decided to name the place Cat Skull Camp. Soon we had that name carved into the thick bark of one of the giant nearby fir trees.

About this same time a cult leader by the name of Norman "Snake" Brooks had also been using the Siuslaw drainage, but for entirely different purposes. Brooks and eighteen female companions had been evicted from a cabin on the upper Siuslaw in 1972 and had later returned to live in a cave in the upper Siuslaw area below Lorane. I had run into this group the previous summer while scouting for fur sign just above the falls of the river.

I was returning down a remote and narrow dirt road that I had ascended a couple of hours before, when suddenly I came upon several of the hardest looking women I had ever seen. They were busy picking blackberries alongside the road and some were wearing side

61

arms. I had heard all about this clan and knew immediately who they were. Needless to say, I didn't stop or slow down and passed through the swarm of females with only rough stares aimed at me. I breathed a sigh of relief and thought no more about them.

After trapping out of my Leopold Creek camp for over two months, I decided to pull camp and finish up my season by canoe trapping on the Willamette River nearer to home. Due to the muddy conditions of my access road, I decided to leave my truck parked on the gravel logging road and carry my camping gear the hundred yards out to the truck.

I had torn down most of my camp and was busy loading my pickup when I glanced down the road toward where it intersected with the Esmond Creek road. Much to my surprise the road was blocked by a sheriff's car with several other backups parked behind that automobile. Over the hood of the car leaned several lawmen with a bull horn and what I assumed were several firearms casually aimed in my direction.

After a short discussion over the bull horn a brave lone sheriff deputy came walking up the road, while I tried to figure out what I had done to bring on such a serious detachment of lawmen. After a few questions and with some relief on both sides, I explained what I was doing and he explained that they had thought that I might be part of a dangerous cult that was known to be in the general area.

The sheriff had evidently surveyed my camp while I wasn't around, saw the "Cat Skull Camp" sign, and decided it must be the Brooks cult. I received a warning to get a permit for camping in the future. The lawmen and private timber company trucks then dispersed to leave me to my trapping.

One of the women in the Brooks group was later convicted of killing sheriff's deputy Roy Dirks, and spent several years in jail. Brooks himself got off with obstructing justice. I got off with only a couple of good scares and decided never again to carve anything like "Cat Skull Camp" in the trees around my tent.

Bob Gilman stands with a day's catch of Siuslaw River bobcats and a coyote in 1981.

Hungry for Pancakes

It was a typical winter day with strong winds, dark clouds and rain pouring down by the bucket. I was trapping bobcats and beaver in the Oregon Coast Range mountains and had my wall tent set up at Cat Skull Camp. At the end of the day my pickup slid to a stop on the muddy road a few yards from my tent. I grabbed my flashlight and unloaded some critters and placed them under a tarp rigged as a skinning shed. I would skin by lantern a little later, but for now I headed into the pitch black tent.

It had been a long day of driving over one hundred miles of logging

63

roads that formed a spider web of access roads to old logging sites. The mixture of old growth timber and cut over lands provided hundreds of square miles of excellent beaver and bobcat habitat. I was soaked to the skin, even under full rain gear, and the forty-degree temperature felt much colder than it really was. The sound of pouring rain was amplified by the tent but was somehow comforting. I guess many years of living and camping in the heavy rains of western Oregon had conditioned me to enjoy the sound.

It was seven in the evening, a long time since an early breakfast and no lunch today. I was famished. But first things first, so I grabbed some black pitch kindling and soon had a roaring fire going in my sheet metal stove. I placed the water kettle on the stove to make some hot tea. The fire warmed the tent quickly, and as soon as I could no longer see my breath in the lantern light I pulled off the rain gear and wet clothes. It is hard to describe how good a change into warm dry clothes and socks feels after long hours of slogging around setting traps in beaver ponds and on brushy ridges where the cats like to travel in this rain soaked country.

Ever since I had slid to a stop in front of my tent I had been planning my evening meal. In my mind it was a meal fit for a king. Venison back strap from a fall buck sat thawed in my ice chest and all the makings for buttermilk pancakes were in my grub box, a simple meal but delicious and filling. Even before I began mixing the pancakes I could taste them sliding down my half-starved gullet greased with plenty of butter and maple syrup followed by the tender slabs of venison.

I had been cooking venison and pancakes since I was eight years old and figured I had just about perfected this meal. I placed some dry fir wood in the firebox, and the frying pan began to sizzle on the hot cast iron stove top. I floured the thin venison steaks, put them in the pan and began turning them each time the blood began to show on top. I then put the cast iron griddle on the stove and went to mix my pancake batter from scratch, no pre-mix in my camp. Flour, egg, buttermilk, sugar, a little baking powder, a little soda and oh, yes, some cooking oil from the little bottle my wife had filled while packing my grub box.

The tender back strap was almost done, so I slid it to the back of the stove to finish cooking and stay warm as I dropped six large spoons full of batter on the hot griddle. While the pancakes cooked on one side I poured hot water and fixed some sweet tea. Not a motion was wasted as I flipped the golden brown pancakes and pulled the butter and syrup out of the grub box. Everything would be finished, hot and ready to eat at exactly the same time.

I stacked the pancakes high on my plate and put a thick pad of butter between each one, then forked several disks of back strap around the sides of the plate and drenched the whole works with plenty of syrup. A twenty-eight-year-old man who has worked hard all day in wet cold weather without a meal can do justice to a mighty platter of food, and I intended to do my best.

My good friend Gary Black's Uncle Bervon had an old hound dog named Rock, and I remember how he use to slobber in anticipation when food was about to be served. I guess I looked a little like old Rock as I sat on the end of my bunk, the fire having comfortably warmed the tent, my tea sitting next to me, and the plate on my lap filled with perfectly cooked pancakes and venison. I paused for just a moment to enjoy the smell wafting up from the steaming plate.

This meal was worth the wait. That magic moment had arrived as I cut a big mouthful of pancakes and closed my eyes to savor the taste and texture. But my eyes popped open wide and a gurgling squawk came out of my throat as my taste buds collided with —SOAP! — SOAP! I spewed the mouthful of pancakes across the tent floor and looked in horror at my beautiful meal fit for a king.

Turned out the bottle of cooking oil was really my dish detergent. Not even old Rock could have eaten those pancakes. I did my best to rinse that soap out of my mouth but that taste stayed with me for several days.

Well, hunger didn't go away so I fixed another batch of batter making sure to find the proper bottle of vegetable oil. I sullenly forked in my overdone venison and pancakes that had somehow lost their magic and crawled into bed. To heck with skinning tonight, the wind was blowing too much anyway. Maybe it would calm down tomorrow evening.

After a while I began to wonder if my wife might have planned this little mistake? Maybe she was trying to get even with me. It hadn't been too long since we had civet cats in the attic of our little cabin on Kennedy Lane. One night after going to bed we heard a noise in the kitchen. I got my Ruger 22 caliber pistol out and went to investigate.

Something was in the cupboard above the cook stove, and when I opened it a big civet was pleasantly eating a box of Cheerios. There didn't seem to be any choice so I opened fire. Unfortunately, I made a bad shot and wounded the civet who had plenty of time to spray his skunk odor along with more blood than I thought possible in a small animal. I decided to leave early the next morning for an extended trapping adventure while Judy cleaned up and aired out the house. I don't know why she would want to get even with me . . . .

Ever Seen Bigfoot?

In the late 1970s, I was running long traplines in the Siuslaw and Smith River drainages of the Oregon Coast Range mountains. By this time in my life I had hunted, trapped and fished over a large part of Oregon backcountry but hadn't yet had any personal contact with Bigfoot. Growing up in a hunting family, around other hunters, loggers and trappers and knowing how they generally felt about Bigfoot, I hadn't given much thought to the possibility of a real Bigfoot creature.

In the late winter of 1979, I decided to trap the lower Smith River drainage and learn a little new country. At Twin Sisters Campground where Sisters Creek enters Smith River, I set up my wall tent and established a short-term comfortable camp. Few people in those days had the desire to camp in the Coast Range during winter, so I had the campground all to myself for the first couple of weeks. I strung out my traps in the surrounding mountains, mostly around logged-off areas where the new trees and brush were creating ideal habitat for bobcats, coyotes and other wildlife.

One afternoon I returned to camp and discovered someone else had pulled in and set up camp. Later as I finished up skinning, a distinguished looking gentleman about fifty years old walked over to my camp and introduced himself. His name is long forgotten, but he said he was a retired sawmill owner from northern California.

I had eyeballed his camp upon my return and it was obvious that he was well fixed. A very nice newer model four-wheel-drive pulled a high-class travel trailer. Everything looked to be first rate. Our casual conversation lasted quite a while. He was curious about what I was doing and seemed quite interested about my trapping profession.

Eventually the conversation turned to what his purpose was for wintertime camping in this remote area of Oregon. The gentleman explained that he was on an extended trip to discover Bigfoot in this part of the country. He politely questioned me about any possible sightings I may have had of Bigfoot, but I informed him that I hadn't seen any evidence or met any loggers or old-time trappers who actually believed in Bigfoot. In fact, the only way I would ever believe Bigfoot existed would be to capture one in one of my traps.

He looked a little amused at my statement and pleasantly informed me that he had only recently met up with Bigfoot in the mountains of northern California. Not only had he personally seen Bigfoot with his own eyes, but on that occasion he had actually had extensive conversation with the beast. In the conversation with me, he did not say what language Bigfoot used, but I assume it must have been English. This conversation took place in apparent complete sincerity, and I think he actually believed the story he was telling.

After this extraordinary conversation, I no longer viewed the guy as pleasant and harmless, but thought I saw a somewhat deranged look in his eyes. I quickly ended the conversation with the excuse of fixing something to eat and he departed for his camp. As soon as his door closed I started throwing camping gear in my truck and twenty minutes later departed the area for home.

High Flying Saucers?

The old homestead at the end of the pavement six miles below Lorane had been vacant land since Dad and I had first trapped for beaver across the river and up a small tributary stream in 1961. I had parked my pickup dozens of times in the old orchard, had crossed the logs spanning the river and set traps for beaver, bobcats and other fur bearers.

In 1975, I was starting to set a lot of bobcat traps and the logs across the river at this old homestead were a perfect spot to capture bobcats. Early in the winter I set several traps on these logs and up the old road across the river. I continued to check these traps for several weeks and had occasionally made a catch. One day when I pulled up to the old orchard to check traps, I was shocked to see that a double-wide trailer had been towed right out into the middle of the old orchard and a pickup was parked in the road blocking the entrance. A man and woman were busy working on their new house.

I sure didn't like the prospect of confronting these people with the fact that I had steel traps set only a short distance from them, but it had to be done. I stepped out of the pickup with some trepidation which dramatically increased when I got a good look at the young man. He was a very tall red-headed guy and I swear he looked just like Bill Walton, the famous basketball player. The red hair flowed wildly down and over his shoulders, and I could see he was sure enough a hippy.

I walked directly up to him, introduced myself and quickly told him what I was doing and that I needed to pull my traps. I was much surprised when he acted quite friendly and began to ask me a few questions about trapping and what kind of animals I captured. It seemed that he was a little taken with the idea of meeting a real live trapper.

He gestured wildly with his long arms and big hands as he informed me that he had just moved up from southern California and had purchased this homestead in the wilds of Oregon. He seemed well educated and pointed out that he had measured the depth of the loam soil and found it to be the best and deepest loam of any place on the West Coast. He was very excited about the beauty of this remote rural area and emphatically stated that he had been high ever since arriving in Oregon.

I was beginning to relax a little and realized that at least I wasn't dealing with a rabid anti-trapper hippy, although his looks clearly indicated hippy. Suddenly, a strange stare came over his face as he looked me straight in the eyes and ask solemnly if I had ever seen Bigfoot? This, of course, is not an uncommon question to trappers. Many people believe that if anyone would have knowledge of Bigfoot it would be a trapper.

Nevertheless, I gave my standard Bigfoot answer, that I had never seen Bigfoot and had never seen any evidence of one. In fact, I added, I just didn't believe in Bigfoot.

"Well," said the hippy, with that same serious look, "I didn't believe in flying saucers either, until one landed out here just the other day!" His large bony hand pointed to a small clearing at the edge of the orchard, and a somewhat wild look entered his eyes. It came back to me then: "I have been high ever since arriving in Oregon."

I quickly departed his company, gathered my traps and headed down the river.

Getting to Know Big Jim

In 1979, I was serving as president of the local chapter of Fur Takers of America. Chapter 11 was one of the largest chapters in the state and I was getting to know quite a few trappers and hunters from around the state. It wasn't uncommon at all to get calls or visits from trappers I didn't know.

Late one Friday evening, after a long day on the trapline, someone knocked at the kitchen door. When I opened it a large raw-boned rough-looking man informed me that he was a local hound hunter/ trapper who was interested in having me trap some beaver on his brother's large ranch. Trappers and hound hunters almost always look rough, so I didn't think too much about it and invited him and his two overgrown teenage offspring in.

I was always interested in finding new places to trap, so I listened intently as the man described the situation. It seemed as though his brother's ranch was overrun with beaver, so much so that when he tried to run cats or coon on the ranch, the dogs were getting attacked and chewed up by the treacherous beavers! Well, I didn't have hounds, but I did know a little about hunting with dogs, and this story sounded mighty suspect.

Before I could respond, he informed me that, by the way, he had just gotten back from eastern Oregon where he had taken a large number of bobcats this last week. I don't remember the number of cats, but it was far too high to be credible and I was sure that he was "stretching the truth a little." Then he quickly suggested, how about if I would go down to the Sutherlin area with him and look at this ranch —TONIGHT?

Somewhat irritated with this wild story, I asked this fellow what his name was?

"Big Jim McKay," he said.

I'm sure the blood drained right out of my face. I had never met Big Jim until now, but I had heard him cussed and discussed by numerous trappers many times. In fact, two normally calm people that I knew had vowed that they would kill him if given the opportunity. Big Jim had a reputation for almost anything bad.

Stealing bobcats and traps was one of the lesser accusations. I had heard stories of his involvement in numerous game law and poaching violations (from the local game warden), car theft, illegal drug activity, and bank robbery just to mention a few of the outlaw legends. Big Jim was big, tough and mean, if looks and reputation meant anything.

Big Jim had lost his leg earlier in life in a logging accident, and the story was told of how he sang songs and joked with the guys who were packing him out as he almost bled to death. Now he was standing in my kitchen at 9:30 p.m. on a dark winter's night, insisting that I go with him right now to look at this beaver problem on a ranch forty-five miles south from Cottage Grove.

Big Jim was a hound man with a big chip on his shoulder for just about any trapper. At that moment, it was very clear to me that Jim was attempting to get into the trapping business by luring me to a place that I did not want to go. Fortunately I remembered that I had an important something to do. In fact, I had several friends who were supposed to arrive any minute.

"Sorry, I just can't do it tonight, but I should have some time next week and I'll give you a call," I said, with my biggest smile.

Big Jim looked unhappy. It was important to get this done tonight, "The dogs, you know," but to my great relief he limped out the door and departed with his two ruffian sons.

The next morning two bobcat pelts were missing from my garage. I never saw Big Jim again but I heard that he died in prison a few years ago.

Trapline Hazards and the Big Wind of '81

In 1826 the famous botanist David Douglas was camped on Oregon's Umpqua River just above modern day Elkton. Douglas was traveling with a Hudson's Bay brigade commanded by Roderick McLeod. He had temporarily left the trappers' brigade, moving up the wild Umpqua drainage in search of the sugar pine tree. Douglas had been shown the seeds of the tree by local Indians but the tree was not yet known to science.

Camped without "white companions" along the Umpqua River on the night of October 26, 1826, Douglas wrote this description of what he endured:

> Last night was one of the most dreadful I have ever witnessed, the rain falling in torrents, was accompanied by so much wind as made it impossible to keep up a fire; and to add to my miseries the tent was blown about my ears, so that I lay till daylight with my blanket on Pteris Aquiline, (bracken fern) with the drenched tent piled above me. Sleep was of course not to be procured; every few minutes the falling trees came down with a crash which seemed as if the earth was cleaving asunder, while the peals of thunder and vivid flashes of forky lightning produced such a sensation of terror as had never filled my mind before for I had at no time experienced a storm under similar circumstances of loneliness and unprotected destitution.

David Douglas had been camped less than twenty air miles southeast from where my trapping camp was now located some 150 years later. While the circumstances were certainly different, I

73

would soon have a direct connection with the terror-filled night that David Douglas described.

In the late fall of 1981, I pulled into my camping spot on Esmond Creek with plans to set my tent up in the same spot as last year. Trapping season would open on November 15 and I planned to be prepared. I rolled my tent out on the ground and started to position it around the trenches still evident from the previous year. The large Douglas fir with "Cat Skull Camp" carved into the deep bark was only six feet from the front flap of the tent. As I gazed around the beautiful campsite I happened to glance up and noticed a large widow-maker limb about forty feet up this huge tree, directly over my tent. I instantly recalled my dad's sage advice about setting up tents and watching out for snags or dead limbs that might fall. But the tent had been set up here last season without trouble.

I continued to roll out the tent and started to stake it down but that large dead limb was beginning to bother me. I looked at it several times and finally in disgust decided I should move my tent.

Unfortunately, there was no spot large enough in the immediate area to move the tent. However, across the creek from my tent and about 200 feet away had been the old Leopold log cabin. The cabin had been burned down the year before and a small clearing was now grown up in grass. A few old apple trees were still present. Surrounding the cabin site International Paper Company had planted trees fifteen years earlier that were now about twenty feet tall. This would be a good alternate location for my tent, but I had to drive about a mile around to get to a narrow dirt road that led back into the old homestead site on the other side of the creek. I grudgingly loaded my tent and gear, drove to the new location and started setting up camp in the new spot.

On November 13, I pulled into my tent camp at the old cabin site after dark in a pouring down rain. For anyone who hasn't experienced the bone-chilling torrential winter rains of the Oregon Coast Range, it may be hard to understand how good a warm and drying wood fire feels at the end of the day. After removing my sou'wester, rain pants and rubber boots, I built a roaring hot fire of dry fir and alder wood. The night was already pitch black and the wind was blowing with occasional heavy gusts. These kinds of winds are not at all uncommon in this part of the country, and I thought little of the thirty-five mile per hour wind gusts as I fixed my dinner of venison, eggs and fried potatoes and relaxed with a hot cup of coffee.

By late that evening, things had changed dramatically, and the winds were roaring down the canyon off the high ridges of Roman Nose Mountain three miles west of my camp. By midnight I was experiencing the worst storm I had ever camped in. No wind recording instruments are located in this part of the Oregon Coast Range, but as trees started to fall in all directions from my camp I estimated sustained winds of forty to fifty miles per hour and gusts that reached eighty to ninety miles per hour.

Weather records later showed wind gusts as high as ninety-two and one hundred miles per hour along the Oregon coast. The 1981 wind storm was the second strongest wind storm recorded in Oregon since modern records began in 1880. Thunder and lightning crashed through the black sky every couple of minutes. David Douglas' description of his experience was in every sense what I experienced:

> ...every few minutes the falling trees came down with a crash which seemed as if the earth was cleaving asunder, while the peels of thunder and vivid flashes of forky lightning produced such a sensation of terror as had never filled my mind before.

Fortunately, I made the right decision when I moved camp to the south side of the creek. However, when old growth fir, cedar and hemlock trees are crashing down near your tent, a two-hundred-foot move is of little comfort. Of course I survived the night but the destruction that met my eyes the following morning was incredible.

No less than eight of the huge trees had gone down in the stand across the creek where I had camped in past years and hundreds more in the nearby surrounding forest. Many of these trees were four to six feet in diameter at the base and over two hundred feet tall. No trees had fallen across my old tent site; however, that large widow-maker limb six inches in diameter and ten feet long lay diagonally inside the trenches that outlined where my tent had been temporarily rolled out only a few days before. I would never again set up a tent without thinking of Dad's advice and closely looking over the area for snags and widow makers. Without a doubt, wind storms are among the scariest and most dangerous events in this big timber country.

Deadfalls are Dangerous!

As usual, it was pouring down rain and had been for several days. I was camped on Leopold Creek just a few miles from where I was checking traps on Esmond Creek. Bobcats were bringing good money in 1978 and I figured on getting eighty to a hundred dollars apiece for my Coast Range cats. I had dozens of traps set throughout the Siuslaw drainage. Esmond Creek was one of my favorite systems to trap.

I had first hiked into Esmond Lake when I was five years old with Dad and Uncle Jerol. At that time in 1955 no roads went into the lake and it was a four-mile hike through virgin old-growth fir, cedar and hemlock forest to reach the lake. Every pool in the stream was filled with small trout and steelhead. A baited hook would bring swarms of small fish fighting for the chance for a worm. Years later, Al Weekly told me that he and his brother, Dave Conn, had trapped many mink on this stream back in the early 1920s when they had hiked all the way from Siuslaw Falls running mink traplines along the Siuslaw. By the late 1970s, the stream had been cleared of all log jambs by the Oregon State Game Commission. The logging companies that cut timber in the area were also required to clean any logs out of the stream under the misguided assumption that a stream devoid of log jams, brush and general debris would be good for fish.

When it wasn't raining, Esmond Creek could be waded in most places and is normally twenty to thirty feet across with a few deep pools. When the heavy winter rains come each season, Esmond Creek is too deep to wade in many places. Windfalls sometimes fall into the creek and are washed downstream and hang up in some constricted area.

Bobcats were especially thick along the vine maple flats on this creek, so I had set several traps in the area as part of my extended trapline. One day I waded through the dense salmonberry and vine maple to a flat sand bar along this creek to check a cat trap. My trap was fixed with a six-foot chain and hooked steel drag that usually got hung up on the nearest brush and stopped a cat right away. However, this time my trap was nowhere to be found. Heavy rains had washed all traces of the drag marks, and no chewed-up brush could be found to indicate where an animal had been tangled. After searching up and down the creek and through thick brush for an hour, I was about to give the trap up as lost.

I was standing on the sandbar gazing downstream where the water slowed and had a depth of about eight feet. Suddenly I spotted something moving in the water. I walked down for a closer inspection and was surprised and delighted to see the tail of a coyote undulating in the water. The coyote had evidently tried to cross the stream with the trap and drag and had been washed down into deep water where it had drowned. The trap was on the bottom of the stream but the coyote was floating upwards with the tip of its tail just under water. The coyote was near the far side of the creek in water far too deep to wade.

Fortunately, I thought, just a few feet downstream from the coyote a pair of fir logs had washed crosswise of the stream and lodged against the far bank. These logs were both about forty feet long and fourteen inches in diameter. Both trees were straight as arrows and without any limbs. One log was partially submerged and lay flat across the stream with about four inches of wood above the water line. The other log lay perfectly on top of the bottom log with the end on my side of the creek lodged in the sandbar. The other end of the second log lay on top of the far creek bank about four feet above the bottom log.

I perceived no danger in this situation. Walking logs across creeks was an everyday occurrence on my trapline. So I quickly walked the thirty feet across the bottom log using my hands on the top log to help keep my balance. I then knelt down keeping one hand on the top log to balance myself and quickly grabbed the coyote tail. Hoisting the soaked coyote up I heaved it up on the far stream bank that was about chest high.

I was dressed in my usual hip boots, chest high rain pants and raincoat, and even though the brush was very much soaked and it was raining I was still dry underneath. I shimmied back out closer to midstream where the top log was only about belly high, placed both hands on top of the log and gave a heave to lift myself up on the top log to gain the far bank.

In less time than it takes to write one word I realized my log bridge was a perfect deadfall. My first downward pressure on the top log had broken the lip off the sandy bank and dropped the log straight down to where both of my feet were placed. A skilled deadfall trapper could not have devised a more perfect hair trigger and deadlier drop log.

Instant reflexes saved my life. As the top log came down with my hands still on top, I pushed straight back and dropped into the water. The thousand-pound deadfall dropped with a sickening thud into position just a hair behind my toes as they left the log.

I went down into the water to my chest, and with a burst of

I had no idea of the danger that I was in! Illustration by Sharon Davis

adrenaline pulled hard and shot myself straight up out of the water into a standing position on the top log. This happened so fast I remained almost completely dry inside my rain clothes. If I had not reacted instantly my feet would have been crushed and trapped between the two logs. No one was around for miles and I would have surely fallen backwards and drowned.

I grabbed my coyote, and with one quick backward glance, I headed for the pickup and off to check more traps. I didn't give it a lot of thought at the time, but looking back it was a lucky day for me when I walked away from that deadfall. That moment nearly ended my traplines forever.

Willamette Canoe Lines

Almost every year late in the trapping seasons of the 1970s and '80s, I would run a trapline on the upper Willamette River. One of my favorite runs was from French's Market on Row River down to the confluence with the Coast Fork of the Willamette, and then downstream to a pullout a few miles above Creswell. The river is generally mild in this stretch at normal river flows but can get pretty dangerous during high water. I ran this section each season no matter what the water levels, and one year about 1980 we were having extraordinary rainfall. The river was running bank full and to all appearances and in reality was extremely dangerous for canoe work.

For almost two weeks, I had to be very careful to avoid the worst rapids and had been constantly on guard in the high swift and muddy water. Finally, the rains shut off, and about that time the Corps of Engineers also shut down the outflow of Cottage Grove and Dorena Dams upstream a few miles from where I was trapping. The weather turned sunny and it looked as if spring was about to arrive.

It was my last day on the river and the end of the winter traplines. The water had dropped to a very low level, the sun was warm, and not a cloud was in the sky. In most places the water was only a couple of feet deep and in many of the riffles I was scraping bottom with my canoe. The current low water compared with the dangerous high water of the recent past lulled me into a false sense of security. About halfway through the line I pulled off my life vest. It sure didn't seem important as I floated serenely downstream in a few inches of water, the warm sun nearly putting me to sleep.

Just below the confluence of Row River and the Coast Fork, the river split around an island and the water volume almost doubled. At the head of this island and on its east side the river narrowed to about forty feet across. An alder tree protruded from the island out across part of the channel about thirty feet and was about a foot above the water level. I let my canoe drift sideways and bump up against this tree, thinking I would push off and guide the canoe toward the east shore and around the end of the tree.

Just a few feet above this obstacle the water was only inches deep, but as I drifted into the tree the water suddenly was much swifter and dropped off into deep water. I also noticed numerous other trees had fallen off the east side of the island and were crisscrossed under water just downstream of the tree I would bump up against.

I laid my paddle down and with no apprehension prepared to push off the tree and get around the end of it to proceed downstream. As the canoe gently touched the tree I reached out to grasp it, and instantly the canoe flipped and was sucked under the tree. It happened so quickly there simply wasn't any reaction time. One second I was relaxing in my canoe and the next second I was hanging on to a six-inch tree for dear life.

Too late, I realized my foolishness. No life vest, a pair of hip boots on, deep swift water for several hundred yards and numerous underwater sweepers immediately downstream from me. Even though it was warm I had left my chest-high rain pants on out of habit. Now as I clung to the small tree the current had me stretched out downstream and the weight of the hip boots was trying to break my hold and suck me under.

The only thing that saved me was my rain gear and the adrenalin rush that comes with fear. The water was just below the rain pants chest line and therefore didn't allow the hip boots to fill with water.

I hung there for a few moments trying to think what to do. I quickly realized that letting go would be sure death by drowning. I only had one choice and that was to hang on and get over to the island twenty feet away. In a few moments the swift river would break my hold and I knew I had strength for only one try.

With a burst of energy, I pulled myself upstream and right up on top of the tree and ran to shore. I doubt that it was more than thirty seconds between the time the canoe flipped and I was again on solid ground.

I ran to the far end of the island and caught my well-used and battered eighteen-foot cedar strip canoe as it floated upside down at the tip of the island a hundred yards downstream. The paddle and some other gear were trapped inside and I only lost a few traps. A few minutes later I proceeded downstream, a little wiser, much more cautious and very much aware that it's a very short distance between life and death. The life vest was now strapped securely around my chest.

Weekly — Not Daily!

Almost any trapper who has read books on trapping knows that E.J. Dailey was a famous Adirondack fur trapper from years gone by. I knew who he was from many years of reading *Fur-Fish-Game* magazine and Harding's *Pleasure and Profit* books. One winter day while I was checking beaver traps along the main Siuslaw River access road, an old fellow drove up. He was driving an old blue Chevrolet half-ton pickup with a small camper on the back.

This fellow saw that I was trapping and stopped to talk. I usually don't remember names very well but I never forgot this old trapper's name. He introduced himself as A.L. Weekly not E.J. Daily. Al had trapped the Siuslaw back in the early 1920s with his brother, Dave Conn (Elmer Weekly changed his name), and before retiring had worked for several years as a state trapper for the Oregon Game Commission. Part of his job in the early 1940s was transplanting beaver into the upper Siuslaw drainage. He was still trapping some of those same colonies that he had helped start almost forty years earlier.

It was just before Christmas in 1979 when I first met Al and he had just turned eighty years old. After just less than a month of trapping he had already caught over ninety beaver. In the next couple of years we became friendly and Al sometimes parked his camper overnight at my Cat Skull Camp. He would fix dinner and tell stories about his early trapping adventures back in the '20s, but rarely did he share any of his trapping secrets.

A few weeks after our first meeting, I ran into Al one day near Doe Creek on the upper Siuslaw and we talked for a while. During our conversation I told Al that I was trapping as far downriver as Whitaker Creek. I saw a frown cross his face as he told me he had had a trap stolen off that stream just a few days before. It was evident that he was somewhat suspicious that I may have taken his trap, but he said no more. There wasn't much I could say. He didn't know me very well at the time and I was trapping in that area.

We parted after a few minutes of polite conversation and each went our way. I headed downstream toward my camp forty miles away. Later that day I came upon three vehicles stopped in the middle of the road and their occupants were all talking. One of these guys was a trapper that I knew, although not well. The other two guys turned out to be trappers also. Now this was something. Fur prices were high, and competition was stiff, but I had never seen three trappers in one spot and now I was the fourth. I soon introduced myself and entered into the conversation.

One of these fellows who I didn't know was a part-time trapper and hound hunter. He was telling stories and before too long he started telling about finding an old lost 4 ½ Newhouse wolf trap on Whitaker Creek the week before. He explained that his son had actually found the trap and that it had probably been lost for years.

I immediately perceived who that trap belonged to. Al had

described the 4½ Newhouse wolf trap, and they were rare even then. Being somewhat stung by Al's accusing look earlier in the day, I quickly and without regard to politeness told the trapper "whose" trap that was and that it was not lost but stolen!

The man seemed a little taken back and said he would make sure the owner got his trap back. I wasn't satisfied and told him to bring the trap and leave it behind a large boulder that happened to be near where we were standing. He assured me he would do just that the next time he came through the area. I wrote down his name, address and telephone number and departed the pow wow.

I traveled through this area very frequently and over the next month I stopped several times and searched behind the boulder. No trap was ever left and I finally gave up stopping. One day in early summer after the trapping season I happened to run across the information I had written down about this trapper and decided to call Al Weekly and let him know who had his trap. I was still worried that he thought I had taken it. I found Al's number and gave him a call, gave him all the information I had about this guy and urged him to call the fellow and demand his trap back.

The next season, Al stopped by my camp a couple of times but the stolen trap never came up. I didn't run into Al after that for the next two years and was thinking that he had probably passed on to the happy trapping grounds. It was one of those clear, beautiful and rare late winter days in the Oregon Coast Range mountains. I had stopped to eat lunch on top of the divide between the Siuslaw and Smith rivers.

The divide had an extensive view of the rugged Oxbow burn that ignited over 40,000 acres back in 1966. I was enjoying my lunch and soaking in the view when the old blue Chevy pickup drove up and Al Weekly stepped out, still as spry as ever. We had a pleasant reunion and a few minutes of conversation.

As Al got into his pickup and started to drive off, he stopped, motioned me over to his door and remarked casually, "Oh, by the way, you remember that trap I had stolen a few years ago?" "Yes," I said. Al replied, "Thanks for letting me know about that, I took care of it."

I waved as he drove on down the road, wondering exactly what he mean by "I took care of it," but happy that Al seemed to have determined that I wasn't the trap thief. Al was definitely of the old school, closed mouth, independent and took care of his own business. I was relieved that I didn't end up on his bad side.

That was the last time I ever saw the old trapper. He has been gone for many years now. I understand that Al and his wife were killed in a car wreck in 1989 when Al was ninety years old. Most of those beaver colonies that Al helped to start over sixty years ago were still active in the late 1980s, but sad to say are mostly all gone at this time along with the habitat that sustained them.

The logging practices that helped create miles and miles of superb beaver habitat along the Coast Range streams have changed. Many would say for the better, but I disagree. The requirement for loggers to leave buffers along streams stops sunlight from reaching the water's edge. The rich beaver habitat, once so abundant, has now been reduced to a fraction of what it was in the 1950s through the '90s. The ultimate consequence of this change in logging practices has been dramatically reduced numbers of beaver in the Oregon Coast Range. Modern fish biologists sometimes blame trappers for the drop in the beaver population. In the past I would argue with them and try to explain why we now have fewer beaver. It seems to be a waste of breath; they are a hard headed bunch. Now I just say, "habitat and predators."

I also occasionally remind them of how they demanded that all log jams and obstructions be removed from Coast Range streams. These misguided stream clearing activities not only cost millions of dollars in stream damage and repair but destroyed untold miles of fish and wildlife habitat for many years. Increasing habitat and decreasing predators are the keys to increasing the beaver and other fish and wildlife populations in the Oregon Coast Range. My fifty-plus years of experience with beaver tells me that sunlight is a key factor in creating beaver habitat; stream buffers (tall trees) destroy beaver habitat.

A Fragrant Christmas Tree

Three weeks before Christmas in 1978, I was running a long trapline catching bobcats. I had about eighty traps in the ground and ran hard from early morning until long after dark to check and set traps. Many of my cat sets were on the very highest ridges, often at the end of the road where there is almost always an old logging landing. The landing is where a log yarder had been set up when the area was logged. The yarder is the machine that drags the logs up out of these deep Coast Range canyons to where they can be loaded onto logging trucks and taken to the mill.

These old landings are favorite places to set traps, since the bobcats follow the ridges up to the landings and then follow the road on the way to wherever it is that a cat wants to go. The particular landing I had arrived at on this day had numerous small Christmas-tree-size firs growing over about a quarter-acre area. I was using a lot of beaver carcasses for bobcat bait about this time, and I happened to have one in the rig as I stopped to set a trap.

Fresh and old cat scats were evident in the old bark and chip piles left several years ago by the loggers. On the far edge of the landing stood a nice bushy fir tree about seven feet tall, a perfect place to hide a cat set. I went to the back side of this tree away from the road and chopped off several of the lower limbs. Removing these limbs made a perfect cubby with the base of the tree as the back and brushy limbs enclosing two sides.

I then hoisted the forty-pound skinned beaver carcass out of my truck and wired it securely to the tree about two feet off the ground and carefully placed a No. 3 longspring trap and steel grapple hook about sixteen inches out in front of the beaver bait. As a final touch to this cat set I added several good smears of skunk-based lure and some beaver castor to the limbs about four feet off the ground.

I stood back and admired my handiwork. It was only a matter of time before Mr. Cat came along and was captured. The end of this road was miles from anywhere and rarely saw any traffic, but if someone did drive to the end of the road and turned around they would never see my set, since the brushy tree limbs concealed my bait from view. From the road side the tree looked normal and didn't reveal any evidence of a trap set.

I checked this trap set several times but had no luck capturing a bobcat. Late one evening about a week before Christmas, I arrived to check my trap and realized something was amiss. Something looked very different but at first I couldn't figure out what. Then I realized my tree was gone, completely gone!

Closer inspection revealed that the tree had been chopped off at the base. Adult and children tracks showed where the tree had been drug over to a vehicle and loaded up. My trap was still sitting undisturbed just out from the stump of someone's brand new Christmas tree.

I have often wondered what these people thought as they arrived home, pulled their new tree out of the truck and discovered a rotten beaver tied securely to the base. Of course, if they had a station wagon I doubt that they got more than three miles down the road before the rotten beaver, beaver castor and skunk odor would have had the entire family retching alongside the road. I imagine these people always go to a Christmas tree farm these days. They may occasionally wonder what kind of cult would have wired a naked beaver carcass to a tree on a remote ridge deep in the Oregon Coast Range.

Cascade Marten Traplines

I saw my first picture of an American (Pine) marten in a Hammond World Nature Atlas when I was about twelve years old. From the time I first saw that picture I dreamed of someday capturing one of these beautiful and elusive fur bearers. I didn't know it would be another twenty years before I would make that dream come true. Even after I finally captured a marten the desire to capture more just burned stronger.

By 1979, I was a fairly accomplished trapper and was making a living of sorts by wintertime trapping. I was catching good numbers of high value bobcats, beaver, otter and other fur bearers, but marten were a difficult animal to get to. The heavy winter snows of the Cascade Mountains generally made travel by roads impossible by the November 15 marten season opening. I actually had not given marten trapping much serious thought for some time when a chance meeting with a famous Oregon marten trapper changed all that.

In the summer on 1974, Judy and I attended the first Oregon Trappers Rendezvous held at Diamond Lake near the crest of the Cascade Mountains. I had heard of a trapper by the name of Wayne Negus and knew a little about his adventurous Cascade traplines dating back to the 1920s. Wayne and Bobby Negus also attended that rendezvous and I soon met them and immediately fell under Wayne's spell. When Wayne found out that I had a long interest in marten trapping but had never done any, he was more than willing to help me out. Within a half hour of our first meeting we were hiking out of Broken Arrow Campground and following blazes of a marten line of the recent past.

American (Pine) Marten. Illustration by Sharon Davis

Bob Gilman (right) rubbing shoulders with legendary trappers Wayne Negus (far left) and Frank Terry.

As we hiked briskly along an old logging trail, Wayne pointed out the three angled hash marks blazed on trees every now and then. These three slashes indicated a trap location and had been Wayne's mark for many years. The traps were still hanging from the trees, and Wayne explained every detail of how to make a variety of sets for marten and high country red fox. Marten sign was clearly evident around several set locations and before long my marten fever was at a high pitch. I wasn't the first young man that Wayne Negus had inspired to chase marten and I wouldn't be the last.

I have had the opportunity to meet many good and a few great trappers over the years. Wayne Negus was without question a great trapper. Wayne's love of trapping, his never-ending enthusiasm, his story telling, his writing and his woodsman skills put him in a category with few others when it comes to great trappers.

It would be many years before I would be able make a decent catch of marten. The Cascades have usually turned out to be tougher than I am. I did, however, get a good taste of why Wayne had that faraway look in his eyes when he told tales of the long snowshoe lines of the distant past.

In the late summer and fall of 1980, I spent considerable time hiking the high alpine country on the west side of Diamond Peak and around Mount Yoran. Starting at the Notch Lake trailhead I blazed my own trail southeast up into a basin under Mount Yoran and then east several miles up to the base of the mountain. At about 6,500 feet I connected up with the Vivian Lake trail and started looping to the north and west toward Notch Lake.

By the time I had the line laid out it stretched to nearly twelve miles of travel, with the first five miles gaining about 3,000 feet in elevation. It all seemed pretty easy on a cool fall day with clear skies and bare ground. It wouldn't be long before the Cascades would teach me a few lessons on how to get tough quick.

I strung traps and built leaning pole sets, and on the opening day of trapping season I was finally setting marten traps for the first time. I had left home at 2:30 a.m., driven eighty miles, parked my vehicle at the trailhead and started off with great enthusiasm, expecting a huge catch within a couple of weeks. The couple of inches of snow covering the ground made travel easy and revealed many marten tracks along the way. I was able to make the entire loop that first day but many of the traps were not yet activated and would have to wait till the next trip.

Two trips later I had my line all set up and went up on Saturday morning to check traps. I arrived at the trailhead about nine after chaining up all four wheels of my truck and churning up the steep climb of the last three miles to the trailhead. Twelve inches of fresh snow now blanketed the ground at 3,500 feet of elevation. I strapped on my snowshoes and began a pleasant hike up the trail toward my first traps. Within half a mile I was in good marten habitat.

I had checked several traps with no luck, even though marten tracks were numerous. Suddenly, I came upon the fresh boot tracks of an elk hunter who had hiked up a canyon about two miles and struck the trail in front of me. I knew elk season was open but this was unexpected, since few hunters were up that high and in that much snow.

I followed along behind the hunter and checked a couple more traps that were undisturbed. The next trap was right along the trail in plain sight and sure enough that's the one that caught my very first marten. Unfortunately, the hunter decided it was his marten. The trap was missing and a few drops of blood in the snow along with numerous footprints told the whole story. After twenty years of waiting and a great deal of effort and money, my first marten was stolen!

I walked around the tree a couple of times studying the evidence, my anger growing with every step. I glared at the boot tracks that now departed my trapline trail and headed directly away from where I needed to go. I looked up the trail toward my next trap and then back at the tracks of the thief who had my first marten. Without any hesitation, I started trailing the elk hunter fully determined to retrieve my hard-won fur.

The fresh tracks dropped down a steep ridge and headed down a drainage that intersected with a logging road two miles below. I pushed hard and moved quickly on my Alaskan trail snow shoes and fully expected to catch up with this vermin at any minute. I gripped my 22 caliber Ruger Single Six revolver and tried to figure out what I would do when we met face to face. I am normally a very even-tempered person, but in this case the farther I traveled the angrier I became. By the time I reached the logging road, I had lost all reason and was ready to shoot this guy if need be to get back my marten. I can only say it is good luck for me and the thief that when I reached the road he was gone. I couldn't have been more than five minutes behind this guy and that five minutes could have changed the course of my life.

The long two-mile hike up the mountain gave me plenty of time to reflect on the value of one marten pelt. I vowed to never again lose my temper over such a trivial matter in life. Over many trapline years, I have had ample opportunity to test my control in similar circumstances and have only once lost my good sense concerning trapline thieves.

A couple of weeks later, my good friend, Gary Black, contacted me and wanted to ride along and check marten traps with me. Gary is always good company. We had grown up fishing and hunting together and I looked forward to a long day of enjoyable conversation. Gary arrived at 3:00 a.m. on the appointed day and we started the long eighty-mile drive to the trailhead. It was raining buckets as it sometimes does in western Oregon. As we drove east toward the Cascades the rain continued to come down in torrents and the black clouds forewarned of much more to come. Heavy snow had fallen overnight at higher elevations, but a Chinook wind had sprung up off the Pacific Ocean and rain was coming down up to almost the five-thousand-foot elevation by 8:00 a.m.

We hit snow at two thousand feet and chained up all four wheels of the pickup. We churned up the road as far as possible but were still three miles short of the trailhead and the start of my twelve-mile trapline. A more thoughtful person would have turned around and headed home on such a terrible stormy day, but I had every intention of checking and springing my traps. The trapline would then be finished for the season.

I parked Dad's truck, and Gary and I strapped on our rawhide snowshoes for the three-mile hike up the steep mountain road to the trailhead. Gary had no rain clothes along as I did, but the combination of warm rain, steep climb and soggy snow soon forced me to remove

93

mine to my backpack. Within a mile we were both soaked to the skin and sweating from exertion. Warmth was not a problem. It took over an hour to make the trailhead, and it was with some relief that we entered the wilderness area forest where the snow was a little better than that of the road. The rain continued to pour without letup as we slowly worked our way up the mountain.

As we gained elevation the temperature began to drop, and by midday we felt a definite chill even with the uphill exertion. The rain again turned to snow at the 5,500-foot level, and each step of the snowshoe now claimed several pounds of wet snow. Our legs began to complain. We often stopped to relieve the leg cramps, but the raw cold wind quickly forced us to start moving again.

It was 3:00 p.m. when we reached the 6,200-foot elevation, the highest point of the trapline. Here we turned to the northwest to head downhill for nearly seven miles to the truck. A cold wet snow was now falling steadily and our wet wool clothing didn't feel warm at all. We stopped for a short rest at this halfway point and I put my rain clothes back on. I was shaking within a couple of minutes and Gary had no rain clothes for protection. Along with our other troubles our rawhide webbing was soaked and stretched loose, making each step a strain. One of Gary's laces was completely broken requiring much extra effort to keep going. Things were starting to look pretty grim.

Darkness was well on its way and we had several miles yet to traverse. We moved along without much conversation, shivering from the cold and suffering from leg cramps. It was nearly dark when we hit the head of a large canyon where the trail veered sharply to the south. We still had about four miles by the trail but straight down the canyon it was less than a mile to the truck.

After a short conference we plunged off the trail and down the creek, electing to take the shorter but unknown route. The creek at this point was usually about two feet across and less than a foot deep, but now when we needed to cross to the other side it was nearly three feet deep and almost six feet across, running dark brown and swiftly toward a sheer drop-off only yards downstream.

Pushed by the coming darkness and the renewed torrential rains, I took a few steps back and awkwardly jumped the creek. I barely made it and teetered forward to my knees in deep snow. Recovering, I turned to watch as Gary tried the same maneuver. He made the far side with the front half of his snowshoes but started falling backwards into the rushing current. The lacing on Gary's snowshoes had broken and the sagging webs had foiled his jump. I quickly reached out a hand and snagged him, pulling him to safety.

From here the canyon dropped sharply with near vertical drop-offs and large windfalls making the descent very dangerous, but desperation drove us on. It was black dark as we extracted ourselves from the last tangled windfalls and stumbled onto the snow-covered roadbed only yards from the truck.

We quickly removed our snowshoes, fired up the truck and began to regain some warmth through our soaking wet clothing. We were at about four-thousand-foot elevation, but the rain was still coming down in torrents. I had borrowed my dad's three-quarter-ton four-wheel drive GMC because of the deep snow, and all four wheels were chained up. The road behind us went over a high pass and was impassable but the rain had melted the snow going downhill and we would soon be completely out of this dangerous area. We started downhill, and within a few miles were nearly out of the snow and stopped to remove the chains.

A mile later the headlights revealed a fearful sight. The hillside above the road had slid off. Mud was blocking the road and running across it like a slow river. The mud, logs and chunks of debris covered the road for over a hundred yards and the whole place was moving. It was obvious that we would have to make a decision quickly. The road was closed for the winter behind us, it was still nearly thirty miles to civilization and in a short time the road before us would be several more feet deep in mud!

We jumped out of the truck and ran forward into the mud to check the depth. The mud was over our knees and getting deeper quickly, but it didn't appear to have any large logs hidden under it, at least in the first few yards. We found larger logs several places along the road, but a small path just wide enough for the truck seemed to open up before us. We had no time to put on chains so we ran back to the truck. I backed up for seventy-five yards, made sure I was in four-wheel drive and put the gas pedal to the floor. We roared full bore into the mud, spinning all four wheels and bouncing over large chunks of unknown debris.

As we approached the far side of the slide we had slowed to a crawl as the truck struggled against the deep mud. Slowly we gained ground and firm gravel on the far side. We breathed a sigh of relief as we looked behind to see the ever-increasing mud flow getting inches deeper by the minute.

We made it home by midnight and were very thankful not to be walking thirty miles in the middle of the night and trying to figure out what to say to Dad about the nice four-wheel drive truck that he used to own. Supper and a hot shower never felt any better.

I ran the Notch Lake-Mount Yoran line during one other season but eventually decided that I needed a real marten camp if I were to experience old-time trapping. Accordingly I settled on building a tent camp near the summit of the Cascades between Tipponagas and Summit lakes.

I knew this was excellent marten country and began to lay out some eight-mile loops from a central point where my tent camp would be placed.

In the fall of 1985, I set up a good wall tent, roofed it over with a framework of boards and cut a good supply of wood. I strung traps out along the three trapline loops and drove supplies into the camp on a summertime road. It only remained for trapping season to arrive.

Marten trapping camp covered in snow near Summit Lake in 1985.

As usual, good snowfall came in early November and the roads were closed six miles below my snug camp. As luck would have it my good friends and loggers, the Black brothers, were logging right on the road that led to my camp and had kept the snow plowed up to their logging show.

The week before marten season arrived I contracted the flu and a severe chest cold. By the fourteenth I was still sick but improving and foolishly decided not to postpone my trapping adventure. Mom and Dad were drafted with their four-wheel drive to deliver me along with my supplies to the end of the road. Since I was weak from sickness, I decided at the last minute to borrow my brother-in-law's snow machine and a nice sled to get me into my tent camp.

We didn't get an early start and arrived at the end of the plowed road where the Blacks were logging about three in the afternoon. We

The Trip to Marten Camp. Illustration by Sharon Davis

all had a cup of coffee while discussing my coming adventure and I unloaded all my gear along with the borrowed snowmobile. Mom and Dad pulled out about 4:00 p.m., and I loaded all my gear onto a sled that would tow along behind and hopped on the borrowed snowmobile.

I fired up the machine and pulled out as my friends watched my departure into the great unknown. Unfortunately, the snowmobile decided to quit after only fifty yards and no amount of cranking would convince it to start again. With only an hour till dark and feeling pretty puny, I unloaded the snow machine and prepared to pull my toboggan the six miles into camp.

Dick Hess, a former hunting partner and friend, was an employee of the Black brothers' crew. Dick volunteered to take me as far as he could in his four-wheel drive truck and I quickly accepted his offer. He was able to get me a couple of miles closer to camp before the truck spun out, and I again unloaded my gear and prepared to snowshoe the remaining four miles into camp pulling the toboggan.

Dick turned his truck around and departed. As the silence started to close in around me, large flakes of snow began to add to the twenty inches or so that was already on the ground. Darkness was only a half hour away, but the snow-covered road would be easy to follow, even in the dark. I picked up the toboggan lead rope and began to shuffle up the road.

Within a mile, I was running very low on energy, having been very sick and not used to snowshoeing. I soon decided to leave some of my gear along the road to be retrieved later. Over three hours later I staggered up the last slope toward my tent with one small item in each hand. The toboggan and all the gear was strung out for the last three miles along my snowy path.

As I approached my tent camp in the dark, I began to worry about bears. What if a bear had gotten into my tent after I supplied it? It had been several weeks since I had visited the camp for the final time before it was snowed out. I was very much relieved to find everything in perfect order.

I had laid the fire previously so I only had to strike a match. The little sheet metal stove that Dad had purchased from an old elk hunter nearly thirty years before burst to life, and the tent was soon warm and cozy. I fell into bed very much done in and happy to be in my first real marten camp. As I started to drift off to sleep, I heard very clearly the train whistle nearly twelve miles away and recalled the stories of Wayne Negus as he had listened to that same train whistle twelve miles south of his marten camp nearly thirty years before.

As with almost all of my marten trapping over the years, the catch was less than impressive. Nineteen days of trapping produced a total of eight marten pelts. I missed numerous others for the typical marten trapping reasons: deep snow over traps, frozen down traps, marten not interested in the bait, squirrels in the traps when the marten came by, no marten along one whole trapline and pinned down by heavy snows. It's very easy to come up with reasons for supposed failure on the marten lines in the Cascades of Oregon, but the expectation for success always returns the following season.

I love it for the absolute silence of the deep snow country, the complete dependence on one's own woodsman skills, the physical achievement of snowshoeing twelve or more miles in deep, soft snow, the appetite that hard work brings, and above all the beautiful soft brown fur of the marten, just as perfect as I had first imagined as a young boy looking at a picture in Hammond's World Nature Atlas. For these reasons it has always been impossible for me to remember any marten line as a failure. The success comes from finishing the trapline and the memories that come with that achievement.

On the appointed day in early December, I loaded my toboggan with pelts and nearly seventy pounds of gear to pull the ten miles to lower elevation where Mom and Dad were to pick me up. It was a nice clear day, one of only two or three in the last three weeks.

Over six feet of snow now covered my tent camp where I had carved stairs down into the tent entrance. I looked back wistfully at my comfortable camp that had served me so well. It would later be crushed by the deep winter snows, and some of the equipment that Dad and I had used since I was a small boy would be ruined.

I turned and headed down the hill in good spirits and perfect health for the reunion with my family and friends, many of whom probably had doubts about me ever returning. My physical endurance was in top form after snowshoeing for hundreds of miles and I only needed one rest stop in the ten-mile downhill trip.

This trapline had come to an end but the trapping season was just getting under way. I already had plans for setting up my winter cat and beaver camp along my favorite river, the Siuslaw. There was still plenty of time in the year to make up for the early season losses of a "successful" marten line.

After a long day on the marten line.

Boomers by the Hundreds

I met my good friend, Blaine Miller, in about 1974. Four years later we were both at a fur sale in Powell Butte. Bobcat prices had gone through the ceiling and a trapper from Arizona walked away with a $10,000 check for his winter fur catch. Blaine and I struck up a conversation, renewed our acquaintance and spent the day sharing trapping stories. The price of furs caused a reaction much like gold fever in all the trappers attending that fur sale.

Blaine was an expert trapper and one of the best organized people I have ever met. I have done my best to imitate his skills in orderliness during my trapping years. Blaine also had an excellent and valuable collection of antique traps that he had collected and

101

scrounged over the years. Among these traps was one old rusty longspring trap I estimated had value far above the others.

Mac McMullen was a longtime fishing guide and trapper who lived on the McKenzie River near Vida. Mac was one of the best old trappers in the country and in the early 1950s he had been trapping a section of the Siuslaw River just above the falls.

One evening as Mac neared the end of his trapline, he spotted some rusty metal protruding from the sandy soil of the undercut riverbank. On closer inspection Mac realized the metal was trap springs. He quickly dug a rusted bundle out of the bank of six big longspring traps with six-foot chains attached. Every indication was that these were very old traps in pretty fair shape after being buried for very likely over one hundred years.

Mac's daughter later did some research on these traps and determined they were hand-forged Hudson's Bay Company type traps from around the 1820s to 1840s era. Mac had one of these traps still in his possession in the 1980s and would not sell it. He did, however, give it to Blaine a few years before he died and it became a treasured part of Blaine's collection.

Blaine knew of my history on the Siuslaw River, my interest in the Hudson's Bay Company and the value I placed on occasionally touching that trap. In 2001 Blaine gave the trap to me and it now hangs on my shop wall. It will never be sold but someday I will pass it on to someone who appreciates the history it represents.

Blaine also set in motion events that changed my entire life. That change brought an opportunity I had never before considered and eventually gave me a trapper's dream-come-true job. In his pursuit of trapline territory, Blaine had traveled quite a distance up and down the Willamette Valley seeking private property to trap for beaver, bobcats and nutria. He had thousands of acres tied up for his private traplines, much to the disgust of some local trappers with less ambition. One large landowner where Blaine had won permission to trap was Starker

The mountain beaver, also known as "Boomer" or Apalodontia rufa.
Illustration by Sharon Davis

Forests Inc., near Philomath.

Mark Gourley was a young forester who had just gone to work for Starker Forests, and one day when Blaine was in the office Mark asked him if he was interested in trapping mountain beaver for them. Mountain beaver are small rodents, and are not related to river beaver. They live in underground burrows in the Coast Range and Cascade Mountains. Boomers, as they are also called, are found only in the Pacific Northwest and have the nasty habit of quickly chewing down newly-planted Douglas fir trees. This habit is very costly to timber companies and trappers are often hired to reduce the populations in newly planted forests.

Blaine listened carefully, but politely declined the offer, saying, however, that he might know someone who would be interested.

Blaine first asked his sons, Randy and Mike, if they might be interested, but both were starting good opportunities with the U.S. Forest Service and weren't interested in private contracting. Winter was almost over when Blaine contacted me to see if I might be interested in a "boomer" trapping job. Early spring 1980, after fur trapping season, was a slow time for me as the building season hadn't yet got under way, and besides, I would rather trap any day than pound nails. I quickly agreed to go with Blaine to meet the Starker Forests fellow and look at this new type of trapping.

Mark Gourley was a lanky, long-legged fellow with a quick smile, friendly demeanor and a contagious positive attitude. I liked him immediately as we shook hands and rode in his company truck to a place called Norton Hill.

As we drove the thirty miles out into the Coast Range, Mark told a little history of the company he worked for. Starker Forests had been started by T.J. Starker in 1936. T.J. was a highly regarded instructor of Forestry at Oregon State University for over thirty years and had purchased vacant logged-over land that seemed to have little value in the days after the Great Depression. T.J. had vision beyond most people and by 1980 Starker Forests had grown to well over 50,000 acres of some of the best timber producing land in the Northwest.

Upon arriving at Norton Hill, Mark showed Blaine and me the maze of boomer tunnels and numerous newly planted but clipped-off fir trees next to the tunnels. Mark had set a few No. 110 Conibear body grip traps and a couple of dead boomers were held fast in the little killer-type traps. Inspection of these critters revealed a small, plump, short-legged animal about the size of a muskrat or about a pound and a half. Boomers have very short tails, hairy coarse fur, beaver-like teeth and are host to the largest flea in the world.

Mark informed us that boomers caused millions of dollars of

damage to new plantings each year in the Northwest. Much of the Starker Forest ownership was cut over lands with high populations of boomers and Starker Forests was looking for a contractor to work on these rodents.

I told Mark that I was very interested in the job but didn't have any money to start a business, and wouldn't have any idea about what to charge for this kind of work. Mark didn't seem to care about the lack of money and said Starker Forests would help me get started. Their main interest was a good honest worker who was a good trapper.

It didn't take long to figure out that this would be a good company to work for but it would be several years before I understood just how good. As I write this story in 2010, I have done contract work for Starker Forests for thirty years and I believe that several other contractors who began with them about that time are also still working for them. Starker Forests is a one-of-a-kind company!

Mark set up a contract, purchased traps for me, helped with advice on insurance and advised me on what a fair price per acre would be. Then he set me up with the Lafonds, a family of contract trappers who were already trapping for Willamette Industries and who had agreed to show me how to catch boomers. I signed the contract and had my first job with the timber industry.

Mark purchased several hundred No. 110 Conibear traps and gave them to me to use. I told him the traps should be boiled and dyed before use to prevent rusting so he instructed me to take care of that and send him the bill for the extra work.

I lived almost a hundred miles south of most of the Starker Forests ownership, so it would be necessary to set up a camp and go home to my family on weekends. I had already been camping away from home for about two months each winter and now that would be extended by another month or two each spring and fall. I went home, prepared traps, loaded camping gear, said goodbye to my family and

Charlie Mock boiling boomer traps at Knowles Creek in 1984.

headed north to the Norton Hill tract.

After setting up camp in a meadow where the old Ruprecht homestead had stood in the early 1900s, I started setting traps in the afternoon of the first day I arrived. I set nearly fifty traps before dark and had thoroughly scoured about five acres for boomer tunnels. The next morning I started early and, while traversing back and forth on this remote timberland, I set a goal that I never regretted. I decided I would work to become a full-time animal damage contractor for the timber industry. It seemed like a lofty goal at the time since I had never before heard of such a job.

A few contractors like the Lafond Family were contracting for a few months of boomer trapping each year, but no one had a full-time job doing a variety of animal control. Beaver were a major problem in some areas but most trappers did that for free just for the pelts. Porcupines did some damage but very few people had become proficient at capturing these pests. Bears were sometimes a severe problem but the U.S. Fish and Wildlife Service did that work, and private trappers weren't usually hired for that specialized work (I wasn't yet aware of Ralph Flowers and the Washington Forest Protection Association). That changed in just a few years when bear damage exploded throughout much of the central Oregon Coast Range mountains.

Before my second day ended, I had set traps on an additional twenty-five acres of forest lands. After having worked much of my adult life for an hourly wage I could hardly believe my good fortune. Trapping for fur had always been a good experience but trapping on contract was every bit as good. Contract trapping most of the year and fur trapping for the rest of the year seemed to me like a very good lifestyle.

We All Make Mistakes

I continued trapping by myself through the spring, but Starker Forests just kept more contracts coming and I soon decided I couldn't do all the work myself.

Danny Patten was a young trapper from Cottage Grove. He and I had become friends a few years earlier when he and his brother had discovered a couple of my beaver traps and decided to take them home. Dan had just finished his junior year of high school and at summer break in 1980 I hired him as my first employee. Dan was not only the first but also one of the best employees I ever hired. He was hard working and took on responsibility better than most men twice his age. After over thirty years of boomer contracting, Dan still holds the record of over ninety traps set while working alone on a hot dry August day in the summer of 1980.

I first met Danny under less than ideal conditions. I was running a canoe trapline from French's Market on Row River just east of Cottage Grove, down Row River to the Willamette River and then on to a small park below Saginaw. This line was about twelve miles of river and was always one of my most productive traplines. My longtime friend, Mike Bush, had told me that a couple of youngsters were trapping below their house on the Willamette right where Row River and the Willamette converge. I had a few traps set in that area but so far had seen no signs of other trappers.

One day while running my line, I stopped to check a beaver trap on a peninsula where the two rivers converged. The trap was missing and two different sizes of kids' boot tracks were clearly visible in the sand all around the area. Just downstream another trap was also missing and the same tracks marched across the sand to the west. I looked up the hill a few hundred yards directly at the house where the two young trappers lived that my friend had told me about.

I fumed about the loss of my traps the rest of the day as I paddled down the river and considered the best way to get even with the rotten little thieves. Judy and the kids picked me up at dark which was our normal routine. After unloading and taking care of the fur I looked up the phone number of the Patten family and called. I didn't know any of the family at the time but the mother, Enid Patten, answered the phone.

Without any ceremony I told her that her sons had stolen two of my traps that day and that I wanted them returned. She fiercely defended her boys but I was sure of myself and didn't back down. We argued strongly for several minutes and Enid called her boys to the phone where they both denied taking my traps. The call finally ended with Enid saying her boys would not take something that didn't belong to them.

I was still standing by the phone less than a minute later when the phone rang. It was Enid Patten. She said the boys had something to say to me. Danny got on the phone and confessed to taking my traps and said they would return them tomorrow.

I never did hear what Enid said to her sons but whatever it was it got a quick response. I was still a little mad but feeling much better about getting my No. 14 Onieda jump traps back and arranged for the Patten boys to meet me the next day as I ran my traps.

As I contemplated what to do when I met these boys, I remembered when I had first started trapping with Dad. We were hiking up Sandy Creek behind Mill Camp to find a place to set some beaver traps. I had never seen another trapper or traps in the woods, but as we checked out an old beaver dam we found a No. 4 Newhouse trap set on the beaver crossover slide. No footprints or other signs of people could be seen and I assumed that the trap had been there for years. I tried my best to get Dad to take it but he said it probably belonged to some other trapper and we moved on to find a place to set our trap.

We hadn't gone more than a hundred yards down the creek when we met an old trapper in hip boots coming up to check his traps. He introduced himself as Bill Gilham and he lived up by Cottage Grove Lake. I didn't know it at the time, but Bill was one of the top trappers in this area. I met Bill several times in later years while out on the trapline and he always treated me with respect and friendship. He knew perfectly well that Dad and I had looked over his trap and had not bothered it. It felt good to be respected by a trapper like Bill, but what he didn't know was that I wanted to take that trap. Dad did what was right and taught me a good lesson.

I was now having second thoughts about the Patten boys. They were just regular kids who had made one mistake. Had I been alone that day when Dad and I discovered Bill Gilham's trap, I would have taken that trap. I soon decided that I didn't need to set myself up as morally superior to these kids.

After some thought I gathered several old trapping magazines, some catalogs from trapper suppliers, a book about trapping and an application to join our trapper organization. Later the next day as I paddled into the confluence of Row River and the Willamette, two young boys stood on the far bank with stony faces. I jumped out of my canoe and introduced myself to the boys and thanked them for bringing my traps back. I then gave them the information on trapping and some quick instructions on how to set traps. The boys soon lost their stony faces and I invited them to our next trapping meeting.

Dan and Jim had learned a good lesson about stealing but I had also learned a good lesson in life. It would have been easy to create enemies over one bad decision, but by taking a positive approach we became good friends.

Enid Patten also became a friend and told me years later that by my actions I had had a far greater impact on Danny and Jimmy than I realized. I still talk with Danny occasionally. He is now a husband and father. I thank him for allowing me to tell this story even though it is still a little embarrassing to him after thirty-plus years. Dan told me recently that the reason he and Jimmy took my traps was to try and run me off "their" trapline. Danny and Jimmy weren't the first trappers to consider ownership of a trapline or the last to try and run me off.

This talk of trapline morality and ownership has reminded me of a discussion I once had with a trapper who walked into my eastern Oregon trapping camp and informed me after few preliminaries that this was "his" cat trapping area. He did quickly add that you couldn't keep anyone from trapping wherever they wanted on public lands, however, if a person had any "morals" they would trap someplace else. He also informed me that he had recently had a cat stolen from one of his traps in the area. It was clear after a few minutes of conversation that intimidation and a little accusation were part of a plan to keep me and my trapping partner from trapping cats in "his" area.

I wasn't surprised at this visit, since I had already heard of this trapper's imagined "ownership" of the public lands for many miles around. Later conversations with some locals confirmed that this guy was well known for informing everyone that this was "his" area.

I informed the young man that even though I was camped close by I was actually trapping for cats over fifty miles away. He quickly thanked me for not trapping in "his" area. He misunderstood. He seemed to think that I had moved my traps out of this area because it was "his." I had made my decision on where to trap based simply on scouting and current cat sign and had never considered him in the equation. I was a little miffed at his weak attempt at intimidation but I kept my thoughts to myself.

I wondered what would happen if a guy walked into someone's elk hunting camp on public land and informed them that this was his area and if they had any "morals" they would go someplace else to hunt. I didn't tell this guy that old trappers don't respond well to intimidation or that I was trapping a respectable number of cats each season before he was old enough to set a bobcat trap. I also didn't tell him about the numerous attempts at intimidation by some real tough hombres over the years who had failed to get the desired results. No, I didn't need to tell this guy anything at all. It was clear that he was the one who was intimidated.

After some thought, however, I came to the same conclusion as I did with Danny Patten. I wasn't any better than he. I had had the same thoughts of ownership after trapping an area for a few seasons, and history has shown me that many western trappers erroneously think that way.

As I look back over the last fifty years of trapping experience, intimidation and competition has made me a far better trapper than I otherwise would have been. The mean hombres and weak-kneed intimidators have just stiffened my resolve. My old Arky Grandpa

Ware use to tell me "the more you stir an old turd the more it stinks!" One might want to consider that old saying before attempting to scare someone who has a few years on you. The rock under the pan, the urinating on sets, the smashed traps, spikes in the road, short setting and stolen fur, to name a few incidences, have taught me to look close, be cautious and work hard.

Like several other old-time trappers who taught me lessons, the "one arm" cat trapper from the coast with the "funny stick set" taught me that even though I thought I was pretty good, I actually didn't know much of anything about trapping bobcats at that time. Yes, I have had those thoughts of trapline ownership but I got over it. I just embrace the competition and try to make friends with them. Friends are a lot better than enemies any day. Enemies can come back to haunt you when you least expect. I would like to see those weak-kneed intimidators crawl under a dry rock along with their trap and leave this old turd alone.

Well, maybe I'm not completely over it, but, as they say, I'm a work in progress. In all truthfulness, the best lessons that I have learned have come from the mistakes I have made and lessons that I have learned from my competition. The pain of failure has always been my best teacher. It is definitely a mistake to try to intimidate someone who is doing a legal activity so that you can have an advantage over them doing the same thing.

In the spring of 1980, a proposed statewide ballot measure to ban all trapping in Oregon was approved for the November ballot. This measure was no surprise since the Defenders of Wildlife organization had been publicly working on it for many months. Once the measure was approved the awful realization hit home. If this measure passed I would lose my beloved sport of trapping along with my new career doing animal damage control. I left Danny Patten to continue work on the boomer trapping contracts and dove headlong into politics.

1980 Campaign
"The Cost of Freedom"

My first action in confronting the enemy was to volunteer to work for our local trapping organization. I was already serving as the Chapter 11 president and state organizer for the Fur Takers of America, which honestly didn't amount to much more than having an occasional fun meeting with other trappers. Since I was self-employed and free to set my own schedule, the Oregon Fur Takers hired Rod Harder and me to travel to all the major fairs in western Oregon and represent trappers. Rod had a good deal of experience in politics and was a good teacher of how best to represent our interests.

In the course of the next several months, I learned some hard lessons about the brutality of politics. But my love of trapping, a never surrender attitude and eventually learning from my mistakes kept me in the fight, even though at times I would have liked to crawl into a hole and hide myself in shame.

My first valuable lesson was in public speaking. I signed on with the official campaign to fight the ballot measure and soon had several speaking engagements lined up. Most were with Grange people or small town Rotary Clubs. I had never been much of a public speaker because I had no desire or any reason to go around making speeches about trapping. Now that I did have a reason, I had no experience. It didn't bother me much that I had never given a speech. How hard could it be? All I needed was to talk about trapping, something I knew plenty about, and answer a few questions. Or so I thought.

My initiation came at the Rotary Club of Sweet Home, a small mill town at the base of the Cascade Mountains in central western

Oregon. My talk was scheduled to last twenty minutes followed by ten minutes for questions. I had no notes or preparation, and much to my surprise, found out that everything that I knew about trapping could be summed up in about two minutes, at which point I ran completely out of words! What was worse was that there were no questions.

This little talk is still high on my list of most embarrassing moments in life. One good thing about humiliation was that it led me to action. Over the years since that time I have given dozens of talks about trapping, occasionally to groups of one or two hundred people, and I rarely run out of anything to say. The reason is simple. Ever since my first bumbling tries at public speaking, I have always been well-prepared.

My next big failure and good lesson was a radio debate with Sarah Vic Kerman, the Northwest Representative of Defenders of Wildlife. The debate was to take place in Coos Bay, about 150 miles from my home. I had never been on the radio before but again, how hard could it be? I made the arrangements myself and drove to Coos Bay on the appointed day. I had no idea what I was going to do but assumed I would be interviewed and asked some questions about trapping.

When I got to the station, Sarah was already there and we went right into the small cubicle to start the show. Sarah was placed in the left side chair, the radio host in the middle with me on the right. The announcer flipped a few switches and grabbed a hand-held microphone that looked to me to be about sixteen inches long and very intimidating. Sarah leaned over in front of the announcer and smiled at me as the announcer held the microphone in my face and said, "Mr. Gilman, you have three minutes to tell us about trapping."

This was unexpected but again, how hard could it be? I had been trapping all of my adult life.

Sarah moved closer and continued to smile broadly. I started in talking but found out that everything I knew about trapping could be summed up in about thirty seconds, with a few long pauses. The announcer held the microphone in front of my face for what seemed like an hour but slowly realized that I was out of words. Sarah then took the microphone and expertly laid out all the reasons for abolishing trapping in the state of Oregon.

After the opening statement, the debate started and I now assumed I would be chewed up and spit out in little pieces. For some unknown reason the debate quickly turned to the subject of mountain beaver, the one subject that I had recently studied in depth. I was able to answer a few of the questions and debate with a moderate amount of success, but, no question, I learned another hard lesson.

One day in late May or early June of 1980, Rod and I were attending the Clackamas County Fair in the Portland area. We had a booth set up in a large building and were meeting lots of people, handing out trapping literature and doing our best to convince people to vote against the coming ballot measure against trapping. It was early in the day and the huge building was not too crowded, but several dozen people were milling about.

Suddenly, out in the isle about fifty feet from our booth, a young lady in her twenties started yelling obscenities at the two trappers in the booth. The entire building came to a standstill and went dead silent. The only sound was the screaming of the young lady at Rod and me. I froze, having no idea what to do or how to respond to this verbal assault. After what seemed like several minutes, but in reality was about thirty seconds, the young woman became silent and you could have heard a pin drop in that large building.

After a few seconds of silence, Rod Harder stepped forward, raised an arm, and said in a loud and commanding voice and with an air of showmanship, "Ladies and gentlemen, I would like to introduce to you Defenders of Wildlife!"

The entire building burst into cheers and applause for Rod's comments, and the embarrassing spell of silence was broken.

This was just one of numerous lessons that Rod taught me on how to turn around public opinion with timely words and quick action. Trappers all over Oregon are indebted to Rod Harder for the years that he spent representing us through two anti-trapping ballot measures, at the State Legislature, and with the NRA and other arenas too numerous to mention. These reasons and others are why Rod Harder in 2008 was inducted into the Oregon Trappers Hall of Fame.

When the November elections came, to the great joy of trappers in Oregon and all over the nation, the ballot measure to abolish trapping was soundly defeated. I had finally learned to be prepared with my presentations, been interviewed on both radio and television several times, taken several newspaper reporters on my trapline and had the great satisfaction of being a part of and seeing trappers win a major battle against the large national animal rights organization, the Defenders of Wildlife.

I had also gained valuable experience on presenting my story to the news media while staying out of the traps, pitfalls and snares that they continually set. Little did I know that these skills would be put to the test again and again as I later accepted a job doing bear damage control for large corporate land owners, making annual presentations about bear damage to foresters employed by some of the largest timber companies in Oregon, being interviewed on television for the nightly news as a trapper for the timber industry and again facing a national animal rights organization headed by Cleveland Amory and his organization, the Fund for Animals.

The big lesson for me was that often-repeated statement, "Freedom isn't free." It takes hard work to maintain the freedoms that so many before us have fought and died for.

A Partner and
Boomers by the Thousands

In the fall of 1980, I was still working on contracts for mountain beaver with Starker Forests. Since early spring, I had set thousands of traps, walked hundreds of miles in rugged, slashy logged-over terrain and caught hundreds of mountain beaver. This was hard physical work and the long days of working alone were starting to get to me. Danny Patten had gone back to high school. I had met a fellow by the name of Charlie Mock at one of our trapper meetings at Don Nichols' house at Canby the previous summer.

Charlie was working for the U.S. Forest Service and had been trapping mountain beaver for them. We had talked extensively about boomers and fur trapping at that first meeting. In late October of 1980, I had a single one-hundred-acre mountain beaver unit left to trap to finish the season, but I just couldn't face it alone. The long summer of trapping and political work had worn me down.

I called Charlie to see if he might be interested in working with me on this last unit of the season. To my delight, he said yes, and came down and worked with me for a couple of weeks that fall. We quickly became good friends and found out that we agreed on almost everything. This venture was the beginning of a life-long friendship, both in work and play.

For the next ten years, Charlie and I worked side by side for several months each spring and fall doing mountain beaver contracts. Charlie had hooked up with Champion International out of Mapleton, and I had expanded my work to include Willamette Industries along with Starker Forests. I would work for Charlie on his contracts

117

for Champion and he would work for me on my contracts.

During these years Charlie and I walked thousands of miles, much of it in the most rugged parts of the Coast Range and Cascade Mountains. We also set tens of thousands of traps and caught piles of the little tree eaters, camping out for months at a time. Much of the time this was difficult, grueling work on steep slippery mountains of wet logging slash, in torrential coastal rains, amid devils club and salmonberry thorns that ripped and scratched any exposed skin. We wore out a pile of rain bibs and caulk boots during those years. Camping was done either in a small camp trailer or a wall tent, and even though the conditions were rough we always enjoyed ourselves.

In all the years we worked together and in the many years since that time, Charlie and I have never had even one bad word between us. Many years later Charlie was instrumental in my rescue after I dislocated my ankle and broke my leg in an elk hunting accident. Had Charlie not been there this could easily have been my last hunt.

At the end of each boomer trapping season we would pack up camp, head different directions to our homes and many times meet again shortly to spend the elk season hunting together. After elk season I would generally get prepared for fur trapping season. For many years during the mid-1970s and into the mid-1980s, this included a tent camp on the Siuslaw River, marten lines in the Cascades and canoe traplines on the Willamette and its tributaries. Early each spring Charlie and I would do some boomer contracts and during the summer I would do contract carpenter work.

In the late 1970s, both Charlie and I were keeping bees and spent a good deal of time talking about becoming commercial beekeepers. We both had about twenty-five bee hives at that time. As it turned out Charlie did pursue commercial beekeeping and by the early 1980s he was well on his way to success. I never did get past twenty-five hives but my trapping business continued to grow.

I'll Make a Woman Out of You!

In the early 1980s, I started doing river beaver control work for corporate timber landowners. I had finally made my decision to no longer do beaver trapping on permit for no charge. It just wasn't possible to make a living any longer by fur trapping so I started charging for my work. I set up my beaver control to start concurrent with fur trapping season. I prefer to do beaver trapping in the winter since this also allowed me to utilize the pelts that would otherwise be wasted and gain a little extra gas money. From an early age I had been taught to utilize whatever I harvested, and wasting a natural resource was not even considered in my upbringing.

Starker Forests lands were my first contract and they directed me to numerous locations where beaver were or had historically caused them no end in trouble by plugging culverts or cutting down valuable reforested areas. One day, Mark Gourley, the reforestation forester, directed me to a good-sized drainage in the Coast Range west of Philomath to do beaver control. Mark offhandedly mentioned that I should stop and notify a landowner whose property had to be crossed to get to the Starker holdings. This property required going through a gate just past the house and barn of this landowner. Mark also mentioned having had some past conflicts with this landowner, so it was important to let him know what I was doing.

Mark described the landowner, and a few days later I went to the area to start trapping. As luck would have it, as I was driving by to go through the gate, "Old Rancid," as Charlie named him soon after this event, was walking up the road on his way to go hunting. He looked to be about sixty-five years old, tall and lean with a hard look about him. He wore an old red felt hat and in his right hand he clutched an old worn lever-action rifle.

I took the opportunity to pull up right beside him, rolled down my window and introduced myself. I then told him that I would be doing some beaver control up the drainage past his place. That was the last thing I was able to say for about two minutes. In that time I heard a string of profanities as I had never heard before — keep in mind that I had worked in the woods and sawmills for several years. However, he gave no particular explanation of why he was directing his maniacal tirade at me. He shortly finished the obscenities with the very emphatic statement, "If you try to go through my gate, I'll make a woman out of you!"

You may imagine my state of mind, first in absolute disbelief at how I was being treated and then with growing anger as he continued to spew venom. As he finished, I had gone past mad to very calm and had no intention of backing down. I quietly told him that I was going through the gate and if he had difficulties with that he should contact the owners of the property who had hired me.

He held his elbows high as he clenched his gun and tried to stare right through me but I would not be swayed. I put the truck in gear and turned up the narrow drive to the gate seventy-five yards away. I stopped, got out, unlocked the gate, drove through and returned to lock the gate behind me. Rancid was still standing in the same spot glaring at me as if possessed, but he didn't say a word.

This, of course, caused quite a ruckus when Rancid did contact the Starker Foresters. I don't know what he told them, but the next morning right after daylight I had a visit from Barte Starker, one of the owners of Starker Forests, and Mark Gourley. They didn't say what Rancid had told them but I explained what had happened and in the end the old guy never bothered me again during the many years I went through that gate.

I did occasionally hear about some big blow-up including the ru-

Old Rancid. Illustration by Sharon Davis

mor that Rancid's wife got in a fistfight with a local logger trying to gain access to his job site. Several years later I was riding along with Warren Jones, the old government trapper who had grown up in this area. As we passed by this property I told him about the incident, and he coolly informed me that this guy's brother was currently in prison for killing a man in a property line dispute, the culmination of a long standing feud on this property.

I guess Rancid was just in a good mood the day I talked with him or maybe he didn't want to end up with his brother. Either way, I didn't get to be a woman and eventually I learned a good lesson. It probably isn't wise to go past mad.

Then Came the Bears

Mark Gourley and Daryl Adams were professional foresters, both young and energetic and working for two of the best timber companies in Oregon. Daryl worked for Willamette Industries and by 1985 I had begun working for Willamette consistently on mountain beaver contracts. I had also started to do some river beaver control for both Starker Forests and Willamette Industries.

A couple of years earlier both of these companies, along with Hull Oakes Lumber Company, had discovered bear damage on their timberlands. In the spring of the year bears were peeling the outer bark off the valuable Douglas fir trees and eating the new growth or inner bark. This new growth has a lot of natural sugar, and in some areas bears learn to eat trees. Aerial surveys and studies of bear-peeled trees in the Pacific Northwest have concluded that bears do millions of dollars of tree damage each year in Oregon forests.

Looking for a solution, the companies contacted the U.S. Fish and Wildlife Service which provided a professional trapper to catch bears on their properties. The government trappers were experts in this business and caught quite a number of bears, but bear damage continued to increase rapidly.

One problem with the government trappers was that they had a vast area of responsibility that also included coyote control on dozens of farms and ranches in the county. This responsibility caused some irritation since the timber companies wanted someone who would work full-time during the tree-peeling season. Bears usually start peeling trees in mid-April in the lower elevations of the Coast Range and continue until the middle of July in the higher elevations of the Cascades when the trees start to harden up.

While I was doing boomer contract work for Willamette and Starker Forests in 1985, Daryl and Mark approached me about doing some bear control work for their companies. It didn't take long for me to answer that question since there wasn't anything I would rather have done at the time. Trapping bears was the ultimate experience for a trapper and it surely worked into my long-term plan of becoming completely employed year-round as a trapper. Up until this time I had still been doing some construction work during the summer but was mostly trapping for a living.

Willamette Industries and Starker Forests got together with Hull Oakes Lumber Company and formed a cooperative group. This group paid money to the U.S. Fish and Wildlife Service to support a bear damage control program for three months in the summer of 1986.

In the late winter of 1985, I filled out an application with the Fish and Wildlife Service and was interviewed by Ernie Geese who had oversight of the government trappers in this part of western Oregon. I got the job and was soon making plans to start work in early April of 1986.

During the winter of 1985, I had spent much of the season away from home. I had camped in the high desert to trap coyotes in eastern Oregon, tent camped in the Coast Range mountains for bobcats and beaver, spent three weeks camped alone in a remote snowbound area near Summit Lake in the Cascades trapping for marten, and then canoe trapped near the end of winter on the upper Willamette River. I then packed up my camping gear and headed north to the Alsea area for a new adventure and to learn how to trap bears.

I received my first instructions on bear trapping from Ernie Geese and Warren Jones from Fish and Wildlife. After proper instructions Ernie supplied me with a few Aldrich foot snares that were the tool of choice for catching bears. Unlike the old-style bear traps with powerful springs and toothed jaws, the foot snare was not dangerous to people and any non-target animals that were captured could be released. The foot snare was activated by a spring that caused a 3/16-inch airplane cable loop to tighten up around the foot of the bear. After activation the spring would fall away and the bear was captured by the cable which was usually tied to a log drag or fastened directly to a tree.

Ernie showed me the Fish and Wildlife Service method that consisted of building a large cubby or crib. This was simply a large V-shaped enclosure with a stump or solid backing in the rear with a V-shaped fence extending out for six to eight feet from the backing. The bait, which was most often a beef head, was fastened to the stump or tree backing, and a foot snare was concealed in the mouth of the enclosure. Two three-inch-diameter limbs were placed on each side of the snare loop, and sharpened vine maple sticks were placed in a circle around the snare to encourage the bear to step in the center of the loop. If the bear stepped in the loop, the spring-activated device would quickly tighten the snare loop around the foot.

This method of trapping bears had some major drawbacks and was very labor intensive. It was often difficult to find a proper backing for the crib, and the trapper spent a lot of time looking for just the right location to build the cubby. If you didn't have proper backing the bear would often come in from the backside and steal your bait without getting caught.

Another problem was that after a beef head had been out in warm weather for several days it was infested with thousands of maggots. These maggots would fall off the head and migrate out of the crib toward the snare. Voles would get under the trigger of the snare to feast on these maggots and would pack dirt solidly under the snare trip lever. When a bear later came along and stepped on the trigger, it would not go off.

Also challenging was that it took a least an hour, if not two, to build a good quality crib, and when a bear was captured it would often destroy the crib completely. I remedied this situation by tying the snare to a log drag so the bear could get away from the immediate area. In the long run this didn't turn out to be a very good remedy. We were salvaging all the bear meat, and I ended up packing several of the big brutes out of the bottom of a canyon a quarter to a half a mile from where I had originally captured them. Eventually I came up with a completely different type of set and tied the bear solidly to a nearby tree.

The Washington "Bear Man"

In the late winter of 1985, I met an extraordinary man, Ralph Flowers, "The Bear Man of Washington." I had not heard of Ralph until shortly before this time, but he was well known by professional foresters throughout the Northwest timber industry. Ralph was the supervisor of the Animal Damage Control Program for the Washington Forest Protection Association in Washington State.

When I first met him he was nearing retirement after twenty-eight years with the WFPA. Our fledgling Oregon bear cooperative had set up a field tour of bear damage and Ralph was invited down from Washington to give snaring instructions and impart some of his hard-earned wisdom. Ralph was a mild, soft-spoken man who didn't much fit the image of one of the world's foremost bear trappers. He had his beginnings as a local bear hunter, and over many years had earned recognition with extreme determination and hard work as the timber industry's top bear expert. Ralph's expertise had also been recognized in Japan and Yugoslavia where he had traveled to help those countries solve problems with bears peeling valuable timber.

Ralph and I became friends, and he mentored me in snaring

Ralph Flowers, my friend and mentor.

techniques and bear damage management over the next several years. Let me say that being a friend of Ralph Flowers did not put me in an exclusive club. Ralph made friends of almost everyone he touched in life and he touched a lot of people. In 1987, I spent a week with him in Washington observing and learning about his snaring and bear feeding program. Ralph later came to Oregon several times to run my snare lines, critique my methods and be helpful in any way that he could. I was always amazed at the depth of his knowledge on bears and bear damage.

During Ralph's early years of bear hunting and control work he developed still hunting for bears to an exceptional level and took high numbers of bears with that method. Ralph would pick out a stump to set on in some remote canyon where he knew the bears were feeding and simply wait for the bears to show up. This may sound simple but the trick was to know when and where the bears would materialize. Ralph's advanced understanding of bear behavior and his complete knowledge of his vast control area led him to great success in this type of bear hunting.

I also had the pleasure of spending a week deer hunting with Ralph and his daughter, Sylvan, in the far northeastern Oregon. Ralph was a hunter and trapper of extraordinary abilities, and I owe much to him for my success in animal damage control over the past thirty years. Ralph's books should be closely studied by anyone interested in learning about hunting or the habits of black bears in the Northwest.

Ralph's early method of bear damage control focused on taking high numbers of bears to solve the tree damage problem. This worked well if enough bears were taken, but in the good habitat areas of western Washington it was a never ending process of killing large numbers of bears. Ralph later grew tired of killing bears and developed an alternative feeding program that has been in use in Washington, parts of Oregon and even some foreign countries for many years. The motivation for Ralph's feeding program was commendable, however, supplemental feeding of bears or any wildlife brings up an entirely new set of issues that must be dealt with.

One difference between Ralph and me was that I came into the bear control business with twenty-five years of trapping experience. This allowed me to quickly take Ralph's methods and modify them to better suit the type of country where I worked. While Ralph had focused on numbers in his early years of control work and was paid a bounty per bear, I focused on individual bears doing specific damage from the very first bear damage control work that I did. My bear control work was always on a contract and never included any bounty work.

This plan was better suited to the times, helped maintain a higher bear population within the damage areas and succeeded in dramatically reducing damage to the five hundred thousand or more acres that I had under contract for many years. The plan I developed starting in 1986 to focus on specific bears and damage areas was never altered in the nearly thirty years of contract bear damage control that I carried out.

By the time I started doing bear damage control, Ralph was well on his way to developing a major bear feeding program to reduce damage in Washington. The feeding program eventually developed into a well-tuned plan to feed bears during the peeling season and use dog hunters at the same time to remove bears that used the bear feeders but persisted in peeling trees.

At the time of this writing, Ralph's successor, Georg Ziegltrum, had run the WFPA Animal Damage Control program for many years since Ralph's retirement, and I give Georg high marks. Anyone who would step into Ralph Flowers' legendary footprints is a brave man indeed. I am sure that Ralph is smiling down on the job that Georg has carried on in western Washington since Ralph has passed away.

Ralph's favorite type of snare set was the log set. In earlier years loggers had been much more selective about which logs they actually took out of the woods to the saw mills. They felled and left many large "cull peelers" in the woods to rot away over time. These big logs became major game trails, especially for bobcats, cougars and bears. Ralph would put considerable effort into locating a log that could be used for a trail set.

These sets were deadly and Ralph took high numbers of bears over the years in this type of set. Unfortunately for me, those types of big old rotten logs did not exist in my trapping area. Modern logging techniques called for removing almost all logs from the woods, often burning everything that was left. The result was young stands of small timber being peeled by bears in areas with little or no ground cover, much less large logs lying around. It was necessary for me to develop a different method. I quickly decided that cribs or bear cubbies, as shown to me when I first started with the U.S. Fish and Wildlife Service, were just too time consuming and labor intensive. After my trip to Washington and spending time with Ralph, it was apparent that a trail set of some sort would work best for capturing bears in my area.

Over the next several years, and with the help of several of my employees, we developed a baited trail set that was a deadly way of capturing bears. In the early years, beef heads and sheep hides were the primary baits. Later on I used beaver carcasses and would purchase as many as 500 per season to use in our damage control work. In some years I had up to seven seasonal employees and we went through a lot of bait.

One year, we were struggling to capture bears that had become wise to our style of trapping. My longtime friend, Dave Vann, was working for me at the time and he began to develop a sweet bait to use with our snare sets. Eventually Dave's bait was developed into a small package that took the place of the larger meat baits and made the job of bear trapping much easier.

I had also been developing lures or scents to use for bears. These lures and Dave's bait proved to be an extremely efficient and successful way of capturing bears. Unlike meat-based baits, the sweet bait allowed us to continue snaring bears even after the huckleberry and salal flowers came on. These flowers provide good early season grazing for bears and the bloom can be extensive during some years.

The Alsea Bear Job

Nineteen-eighty-six was my first year of bear damage control as a seasonal employee of the U.S. Fish and Wildlife Service. The first season, I parked my little camp trailer at the North Fork of the Alsea Fish Hatchery. This was a good camp with a restroom and shower, electricity and a freezer to store bait and dispatched bears.

Retired government trapper Warren Jones had also been hired to do control work in another area of Willamette Industries ownership about forty miles to the north of my area. Warren had many years of experience, and I spent a few days with him in the Blackrock area setting snares and getting some pointers on how to capture bears.

My general control area started at Philomath and went west on Highway 34 as far as Fall Creek on the Alsea River. The line went north up Fall Creek past the Fall Creek Fish Hatchery and up to Clemens Road. From there the line went west and included the Scott Creek drainage that Willamette Industries owned. From here the line went generally north to Harlan, up to Burntwoods and back to Philomath on Highway 20. My area of control included all the Willamette, Starker and Hull Oakes ownerships within these boundaries.

Dead trees from past bear peeling and fresh peeled trees were abundant throughout the control area. Tree plantations from twelve to twenty years old had the most extensive damage, and stands that

Bear Tree. Illustration by Ralph Flowers

had been pre-commercially thinned were the most susceptible to fresh peeling. The bears seemed to always be attracted to the fastest growing and best trees in a stand. It was not uncommon to find twenty to thirty percent of the trees in a stand killed or severely damaged in a two-year period. The cost in lost timber for the owners of this land was tremendous and they were serious about controlling the damage. Later annual surveys by the Oregon Department of Forestry indicated that Oregon bear damage to trees was sometimes over ten million dollars per year.

Before the snaring season started, I had made arrangements with Allen Ross at The Farmer's Helper butcher shop in Harrisburg to save beef heads that I would use as bait to capture bears. The butcher shop was about forty miles from my camp, right on the road that I took to go home each weekend. The mobile slaughter truck went out on Thursday and Allen would throw all the beef heads into a fifty-gallon barrel for me to gather up on Monday morning. Suffice to say that as the weather warmed up those heads were mighty ripe after four days in a barrel. I loaded the heads in my truck and stored them in the hatchery freezer until I needed to use them for bait. Each snare location usually took one beef head for bait.

I quickly went to work and set snares in every area where I found fresh bear peeling. I set every snare that the Wildlife Service gave me and soon had all thirty-six snares out. My first bear, an adult male, was captured near fresh peeling at Cherry Tree Corner on Willamette Industries land

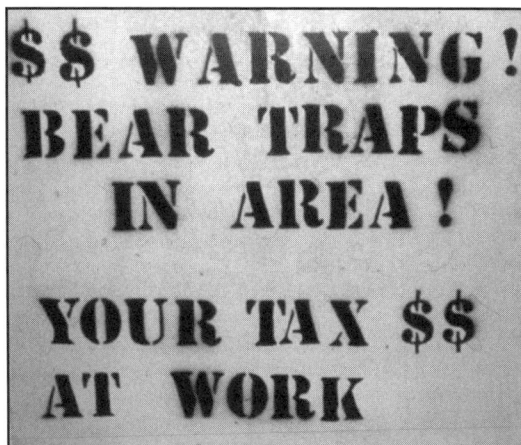

$$ WARNING!
BEAR TRAPS
IN AREA !

YOUR TAX $$
AT WORK

Bob Gilman loads a bear into the truck.

near Grass Mountain. Within a few weeks I had captured twelve bears, and the prospects looked very good for catching many more before the peeling season ended about the first of July.

One Monday morning in late April, I was coming from home to check snares in the Alsea area. At the summit of the Coast Range mountains on Highway 34 west of Philomath, a four-foot-by-four-foot yellow

133

sign with black lettering stated, "Warning Bear Traps in Area, Your Tax $$ at Work." About every half mile I found another sign, all secured to telephone poles and placed high above the ground with climbing spurs. Hard to say who was responsible, although I knew the leader of a local hound-hunting group worked for the telephone company.

I removed all the signs I could get to, but it was too late and they had had the desired effect. The newspapers already had the story which was picked up by AP and quickly crossed the nation. Stories about trapping bears make good print and the news organizations quickly capitalized on this issue.

News of our bear-snaring program quickly made it to the Wall Street Journal, New York City and Cleveland Amory, the leader of Fund for Animals. The famous rescuer of Grand Canyon burros soon had his sights trained on the courthouse in Corvallis. The main targets were the U.S. Fish and Wildlife Service and the timber companies doing the control work. As the trapper doing the field work, I was squarely in the middle of the fight.

During this first season of bear snaring there was some controversy over what to do with the bear carcasses. All parties agreed that they should not be wasted, and finally the decision was made to freeze them in the hatchery freezer for later delivery to a Wildlife Rehabilitator in the Grants Pass area. This rehabilitator would then utilize the carcasses to feed the animals that he had in captivity.

At the beginning of this court action, the news media did their best to get pictures of these bear carcasses, but failed in the attempt. The following year a plan was made to have all the bears butchered and given to the local missions or food banks. Since this plan was adopted many years ago, the bears have been butchered and used for human consumption. Many tons of bear meat have been processed and delivered to the missions in the last twenty-eight years.

At that time the people I was working for had no idea that I had any experience with the news media. Nevertheless, I was quickly chosen as one of the on-camera spokesmen for bear snaring. A couple of things seemed to make me uniquely qualified for the job. First, I didn't work for the timber industry; I was a seasonal employee for the U.S. Fish and Wildlife Service. Secondly, this was my first few weeks with the Fish and Wildlife Service, so they could easily point out that they barely knew me. Should I make some silly on-camera mistake, I could easily be dismissed.

As it turned out, the animal rights people did me the biggest favor they could have done. The lawsuit filed to stop bear snaring brought the spotlight directly on me, and suddenly many people in the timber industry knew me by my first name. I quickly became the bear snare and bear damage tour guide to newspapers and television reporters. Fortunately, my previous media experiences helped keep me out of trouble and my mistakes on camera were minor. The lawsuit was thrown out of court, Cleveland Amory got the media attention that he wanted, and I was well known throughout the largest industry in the state of Oregon.

One television interview during this time was most memorable to me and was a good lesson in how the media works hard to get the story that suits them. In my earlier years of dealing with the news media, I had assumed they were trying to get the facts and I did my best to give honest, clear answers to their questions. Later on I learned that was not always the case. Some media people who have interviewed me did not want to get the facts but were looking for a direct quote that fit their story. In most cases that story already seemed to be written, usually not in a favorable light toward trappers.

I recall one published interview by a news reporter that included two partial sentences cut and pasted together. The sentences I spoke were originally on two completely different subjects in different conversations. I had said the words but the chopped statement had no relationship to what I was originally talking about. More often

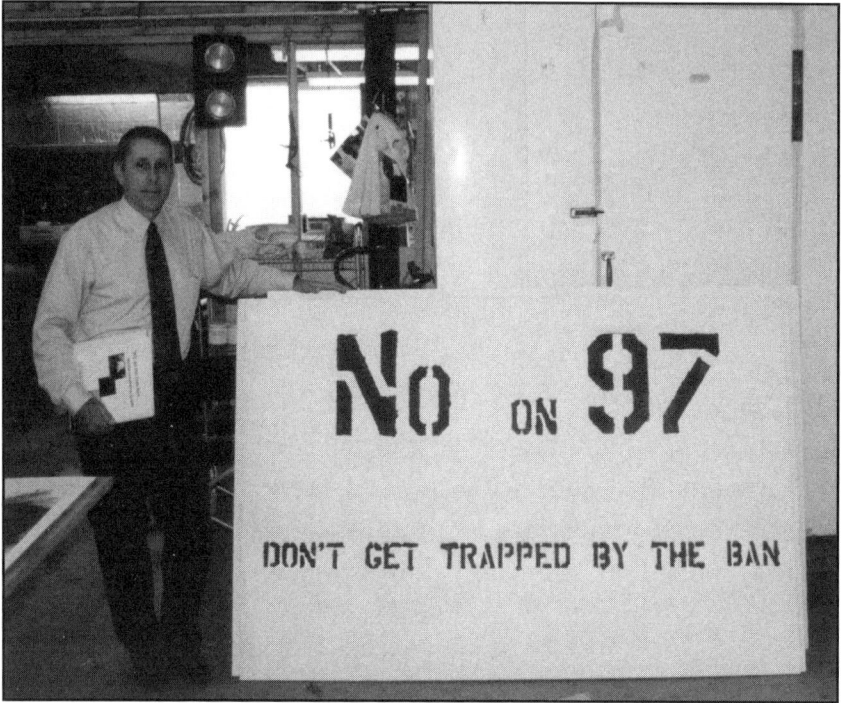

Bob Gilman during the 2000 anti-trapping measure campaign.

I have found that the reporter just leaves out anything that makes sense and quotes something that sounds rather foolish.

During the Cleveland Amory debacle I experienced a classic example of the unethical and dishonest tactics of some reporters. A prominent Portland area television station requested a bear damage tour and interview for their nightly newscast. The companies I was working for decided to okay the tour, and I was given the task of showing them some freshly peeled trees and answering some questions about bear damage.

One important aspect of this interview was to show that bear snares are not dangerous to people. "Bear trap" for many people dredges up images of giant steel-jawed traps with teeth like you might see in a cartoon. The truth was that I was using the Aldrich foot snare that posed no danger to people or pets and is widely used around the world to humanely capture bears, tigers and other animals for scientific studies. A demonstration was in order and that was my plan for this tour.

It happened that I had just talked to Ralph Flowers who had recently given a tour to this same news reporter looking at the bear feeding program Ralph had instituted in Washington State. I was fully informed of Ralph's program and also aware that the animal rights crowd was trying to promote bear feeding as the alternative to killing bears.

The much anticipated big day finally came, and the media crew and foresters headed out in vans to the woods where I had located some fresh bear peeling in a twenty-year-old stand of Douglas fir. I marched the film crew, reporter and foresters down the hill to give them a little flavor of what the terrain and bear snaring were really like. The cameraman seemed to enjoy the tour, and Peter the newscaster was amiable and friendly in his conversations.

After the cameraman got some good footage of the bear peeling it was time for a demonstration of the bear snare. As I prepared to set the snare, Peter the reporter suggested that we do a dry run before filming to see how it would go. It sounded like a good idea so I began setting the snare as Peter asked a couple of questions about the mechanics of the snare.

He then asked his primary question: "Is snaring the best method for capturing bears that are peeling trees?"

I answered that indeed this was the best and most effective tool for capturing bears. I was also careful to point out that these snares were not dangerous to people in any way. I demonstrated this by sticking my hand in the snare loop, depressing the spring trigger and capturing my arm as if it were a bear's foot. This made a nice action shot for the camera, and it was obvious to everyone present that this tool had no relationship to the old-time dangerous steel bear traps.

"Perfect," said Peter. "That's just right. Now let's do it again for the live take."

As I started resetting the snare for the camera, Peter asked me his primary question again for the actual take on camera. However, this time the question was: "Is snaring the only method for controlling bear damage to trees?"

I have made my share of poorly-worded statements and goofy answers to reporters over the years, but this time it was clear even to an unsophisticated trapper that this was a different question that required a different answer.

"No, it isn't the only method being used to control bear damage," I said. "For instance, foresters in Washington are using supplemental feeding to try and control bear damage, hounds are another method used in lethal control, and foresters in Oregon are testing different silva cultural methods to try and reduce bear damage along with lethal control."

This wasn't the quote Peter needed to set Oregon methods of controlling bear damage against those used in Washington, but I doubt that deterred him. I don't recall if they used my answer on the evening news, but I suspect they didn't. If that report went like most other news reports, they just cut my voice and talked over me, while they showed the mean old trapper demonstrating how to capture and kill bears on a split screen shared with a cute little cub teddy bear frolicking in the woods.

In the twenty-eight years of our cooperative bear damage control work, I am most proud of the fact that we have been selective to specific bear damage and stayed away from capturing bears just to produce numbers that may look good when put on paper. This is a great temptation in the wildlife control business. When it comes to bears, the focus of the trapper/agent and the client should always be on reducing the damage and not on catching large numbers of animals. I believed at the time of that interview and still do that selective capture of individual peeling bears is the best way to reduce bear damage with the least impact on the overall bear population.

In the long term, feeding bears to reduce peeling without lethal control does not work. It just creates more problems. I am reminded of a little sign I saw posted on a tree in rural British Columbia: "A FED BEAR IS A DEAD BEAR!" Usually when state or federal government agencies try to carry out Ralph Flowers' well-thought-out bear management feeding/damage control program they mess it up completely. As Ralph once told me while we were in the woods looking at his bear feeders, "Bear feeding works best in an area that has already had lethal control through snaring and hunting."

I have personally observed three programs in Oregon where the feeding program failed and I had to capture those bears that had become accustomed to being fed by humans. The government agencies in charge simply tried to protect all the bears at the feeding stations instead of following Ralph's plan to remove the habitual tree peelers. Those programs eventually failed.

In 1987, I again worked a temporary summer job for the government. The job was now transferred to U.S. Department of Agriculture (USDA), Animal Plant and Health Inspection Service (APHIS). This year the timber companies decided not to snare bears but to postpone snaring for one year to gather data about bear damage. I was supplied with a new four-wheel-drive truck, a government credit card for fuel, and instructions to map and document bear damage over a vast area of the Alsea and Siletz drainages. This was like being sent to heaven for me. I spent the entire spring and early summer driving logging roads, walking into remote canyons and being paid to do what we trappers call scouting.

Boise Cascade joined the cooperative that season. Boise had owned the company town of Valsetz, which was central to the area in which I was to work. In its heyday, Valsetz had a population of over one thousand residents. Boise had moved everyone out of Valsetz the previous couple of years and had torn down everything but one house and the old shop building. I moved into this house as base camp in April of 1987 and remained until July of that year. I thus became the last person ever to live in the town of Valsetz, Oregon.

Throughout the spring and summer of 1987, I learned every road system on private cooperative lands in the Valsetz and Alsea drainages and thoroughly walked all of the canyons that showed evidence of bear damage. This scouting paid off in 1989 when I finally was able to do some serious bear snaring. That season I snared in both the Alsea and Siletz areas and took a good number of tree peelers.

At the end of the summer I printed a report, made a presentation to the cooperative and told them that I would not return next season. I planned to quit trapping and go full-time into the building business next spring. Between fur trapping, boomer trapping and bear work, I had been working away from home that year for over 260 days. Judy and I had discussed this and decided enough was enough. The government job didn't pay very well and the stress of living away from home and family had caught up with us. It was time to put family first.

I planned to trap through the winter of 1987 and then begin contracting full-time in the spring, but a phone call changed everything. Daryl Adams from Willamette Industries called me one evening and asked if he and Mark Gourley could come down, take Judy and me out to dinner and talk with us. I had not even considered that I might get some kind of an offer to continue working for the timber industry, but that was what they had in mind. We made arrangements and a few weeks later Mark and Daryl took Judy and me out to dinner in Cottage Grove.

They quickly got to the point. They wanted me come back to work for them. Was I interested and what would it take? We discussed a few options and Judy and I told them we would consider the idea and get back to them with a proposal.

This whole idea threw me into turmoil since I had thought my mind was made up. On reflection I realized that trapping was not just a job but a way of life that I loved. Building houses was just another job. With Judy's blessing I came up with a plan and an offer to the cooperative:

1. I needed enough constant work to move my family to the area;

2. I would require a six-month contract each season for doing bear control and assessment;

3. I had already been doing three to four months of contracting for mountain beaver and would continue that work;

4. I would continue river beaver control work and fur trapping for companies that would give me permits to capture bobcats and other fur bearers;

5. I would work with the cooperative companies to eventually become a full-time employee, possibly under the control of the Oregon Forest Industries Council.

The cooperative quickly accepted my offer since it didn't amount to much of a hard bargain. The only thing I really asked for was one six-month contract for bear control and then I'd go back to what I had already been doing. In return I would give up my building contracting business, sell my property, move my family and start over in a new area.

I had a long way to go in learning to bargain within a tough industry, but the truth is that in the past thirty years these companies treated me exceptionally well and provided me with all the work I could handle.

The Coast Range Bear Study

I trapped hard for beaver, bobcats and other furbearers in the winter of 1987, and in late spring of 1988 I prepared for my first private bear control contract. Throughout the previous winter the timber companies, Oregon State University and the Oregon Department of Fish and Wildlife planned for a bear study in the Coast Range mountains. This study was to determine the reasons bears peel trees.

Bill Noble, a graduate student with previous bear research experience, was tapped for this job. Charles Meslow, professor of fisheries and wildlife and leader of the Cooperative Wildlife Research Unit based at OSU, would be the project coordinator. The goal was to capture ten bears from each of two different areas, one area having heavy bear peeling and the other area having almost no timber damage by bears.

I first met Bill Noble when I went to Portland to pick him up from the airport. We argued during the entire hour and a half drive back to Corvallis. This was not a good start and unfortunately it didn't change much over the course of the next few months that we worked together. Bill and I were pretty much like oil and water. Bill was thirty-five and had gone to school all his life. He was highly educated, slow, methodical, annoying (to me), had never worked for a private company and from my point of view had no practical experience in life or trapping. I, on the other hand, had barely showed up for school, had nothing but practical experience, was easy to get along with (well, maybe) and had been a trapper for over twenty-five years.

The big rub was that Bill wanted to be in charge of everything, including how to trap the bears. The problem as I saw it was that he had never captured a bear or anything else! Nevertheless, Bill was in charge of the study and started preparing to handle the captured bears.

By March 10, I had twenty snares set, locked and ready to activate whenever Bill was ready to start handling bears. Bill prepared, prepared and prepared until I finally lost patience and told him I planned to start trapping, whether he was ready or not. I was scheduled to trap north of Highway 34 and Bill was to trap south of that highway. My area had lots of bears and high amounts of bear damage to trees. Bill's area had a high population of bears but very little bear damage. In mid-March I activated my snares and soon caught the first bear of the season.

It was just before dark in late March when I pulled up to my last snare of the day. I now had thirty-five snares set that had to be checked every day, seven days a week. Large wet snowflakes were falling and cold wind was blowing on the high mountain ridge just west of Mary's Peak on Old Blue Mountain. I stopped my truck, turned off the key and stepped out to check the snare that was about three-hundred feet off the old logging road.

As soon as I stepped out of the truck I heard a tremendous series of roars that sounded like a mad bull bellowing. In between roars was the distinct sound of splintering of wood. It was an awesome sound and I have never since that time heard a bear make such terrifying roars. This bear was mad and there was no doubt about it. I didn't even walk out to observe that bear. I just got back in the truck, dug out my high-powered state radio and called for Bill. Surprisingly, he answered my call and was soon on his way, but it would take almost two hours for him to arrive at my location.

As I waited, the bear continued to roar almost continuously and it grew pitch black. When Bill arrived we walked out to have a look at the rampaging bear that turned out to be a very large adult male.

He was caught in a foot snare that had an extra-long extension cable. This cable allowed him fifteen feet in one direction and a thirty-foot circle around the tree he was tied to. The dark, cold, wind and snow must have agitated him because he was the meanest bear I have ever seen in nearly thirty years of bear snaring. He let us know very quickly that if we got close enough he would kill us, no question. We didn't get very close but sized him up from a distance with flashlights and went back to the truck to prepare the tranquilizers so that we could handle him safely.

After the dart gun was loaded with the proper dose of ketamine and xylazine, we cautiously approached the bear. I walked up toward the bear to get his attention while Bill circled around behind to dart him in the rear end. As I approached the perimeter of the torn-up circle, the bear became silent and backed up to the far side of the circle, thirty feet away. I had my 44 Magnum drawn and pointed at the bear and stood two feet outside the limit of the bear's reach.

While Bill was circling, my plan to get his attention suddenly worked to perfection as the big brute charged toward me! If you haven't had a 350-pound mad bear charge you in the dark, I can tell you it happens quick and activates all of your senses!

I had been unable to move out of my tracks before the bear hit the end of the trap cable and did a somersault so close to me I thought I felt his hot breath. The old boar had moved so quickly that he had retreated and was starting a second charge before I had time to react and run back to a safer distance.

This bear really had the adrenaline pumping and, as I recall, it took four doses from the dart gun to finally put him on the ground. After the bear was tranquilized, Bill and I worked quickly to extract a tooth for aging, draw blood, put in ear tags, administer antibiotics and put on a radio collar before he came out of the drugged state. As we struggled to get the collar around his huge neck I straddled the bear's back while Bill worked feverishly at installing the bolts that hold it on.

Midway through this process the bear suddenly came to life and lifted me up what felt like two feet, but was probably no more than six inches off the ground as it tried to get up! I bailed off one way and Bill went the other as we tried to get out of reach of the bear. We dropped our lights and had a few moments of excitement before we realized the bear had fallen back to the ground and was now only able to move its big head around. One more dose of hand-injected drugs did the job and we finished our work and left the area just after midnight.

We came back the next morning to check and, sure enough, the bear had left the area. A check of the radio collar indicated he was bedded down in a canyon about a half mile away. This old fellow lay in his bed for several days before he left the area, and I sure would not have wanted to run into him during that time. He probably had quite a hangover and may have had bad feelings toward his human torturers.

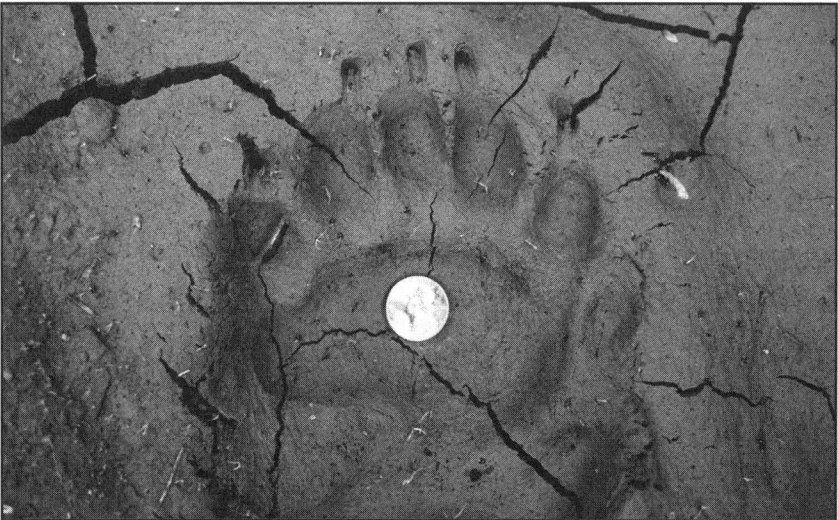

A black bear paw print with quarter coin.

The Professor and Me

Later that spring, Bill needed to take a long weekend and visit his wife who was working in California. Bill had three or four snares out on the south side of Highway 34 and had left me written notes on where the snares were located since I had not been to those locations. The day after Bill departed I went down south with instructions in hand to find his snares and check them.

The first two snares were easily located from the instructions sheet and no bears had visited them. The third snare was supposed to be up a certain paved U.S. Forest Service road "about" two miles according to the instructions. The key to finding this set was one of those little roadside markers that are about three inches wide and painted white. The marker near the bear snare was supposed to be bent over at a right angle about six inches from the top.

After an exasperating two-hour search I finally found the bent-over sign and the related bear snare near the seven-mile marker! I suppose Bill is still laughing about the grief he caused me that day. As it turned out this little exercise in futility turned out to be a worthwhile experience. I got a picture of the newfangled set that Bill had invented to capture a bear.

Sometime previous to this episode I had been telling Bill about an old timber faller who had told me stories about bears licking the chain oil off his power saw when he had left it overnight in one of the rugged canyons that he had worked in. Bill, therefore, decided that a Valvoline oil can would be excellent bear bait and this was the prime draw for the set he invented. The new invention consisted of the back legs up to the hock of a road killed deer nailed to the side

Graduate student Bill Noble searching for bears in the Alsea area

of an old growth fir tree and about six feet above the ground. Inside the legs was a one quart oil container with small holes to allow for a few drips of oil to seep out.

The snare was set up against the big tree with the idea that the bear would stand up to get to the oil can and step in the snare. For those who read this and aren't bear trappers, I will just say the chances of this set catching a bear were very remote. Another incredible thing about this snare was that it was tied to a six-inch fir tree that was not eight feet from a paved road with nothing between it and the road. I was pretty sure at that point that the universities that Bill had attended hadn't printed a manual or taught a course in common sense.

Later that spring, Bill needed to take another long weekend and visit his wife in California. Bill arranged for a professor to take over the work of radio collaring the bears. Professor Bruce Coblentz was not what I had expected; he was young, active and had a history of

Dr. Charles Meslow (left) of Oregon State University and spotted owl fame, and myself get ready to jab-stick a bear. Note that Professor Meslow has my .44 and I have the jab stick! Charles obviously read the common sense manual and was great to work with.

shooting feral goats on South Seas islands. My first meeting with him did not go well, and after years of reflection I suppose it was mostly my fault.

When Bill left the area I continued to check snares and soon captured another bear that needed a collar. I called Professor Coblentz to come and do the scientific work and he indicated that it would take a couple of hours to get his equipment and get to the site.

By this time, Bill and I had captured and collared several bears and had worked out a pretty good system with each of us doing a needed task, so that we could quickly process the bear and get it collared before the drugs wore off. Bill would get the collar ready to put on, hobble the bear, do the measurements and begin the paperwork. I would pull a premolar for aging, install ear tags and draw blood.

Drawing blood was not always as easy as might be expected.

It's the same system as when people give blood, except that a much larger needle is used and the blood is taken from a vein in the groin area of the bear. Finding that vein with the large caliber needle takes some practice, and pushing that big needle into the groin area over and over to try and locate the vein can make a guy kind of queasy. I had learned exactly where to insert the needle after the first couple of bears, but there is a learning curve.

Professor Coblentz showed up after a long wait, and in the meantime I had contacted Daryl Adams, the Willamette Industries Forester, who wanted to watch us work a bear. Daryl showed up with a video camera and began recording the proceedings as soon as he arrived.

I had not met the professor in person until this moment, but after introductions I informed him that it looked like a small bear and we could probably use the jab stick instead of the tranquilizer gun to drug the bear. I offered this suggestion only because Bill always liked to use the jab stick instead of the gun if possible since it was much easier on the bears.

As I quickly found out, it is not proper for the trapper to inform the professor about anything. I believe Professor Bruce had never before worked a bear and didn't seem to be inclined to get close enough to use the jab stick. After looking back on this event, I presume that Dr. Bruce Coblentz did take the common sense course that Bill had missed.

Daryl Adams was filming away as the conversation proceeded and after what I felt was a stern rebuke in the form of, "I will use the gun." Professor Coblentz pointed his finger at the young man with him and introduced him to me as a fish biologist. Very emphatically, he said, "He will draw the blood, he takes blood from three-inch-long fish!"

The implications seemed clear enough to me. My poor relationship with Bill had been discussed with his professor and he hadn't painted a pretty picture. The professor clearly didn't want any of my help or advice.

There wasn't much I could say, so I turned to lead the group up to where the bear was captured in the snare as Daryl continued to video the event. I had taken a quick look at the bear from a distance earlier and thought it was pretty small, however, it turned out to be a large male. This didn't do my credibility any good with the professor but I already seemed to be on his bad side so it didn't make much difference at this point.

Professor Bruce had the dart gun ready, and twenty minutes later he had a sleeping bear to work with. We carried all the paraphernalia up to the bear and the two men started to gather information and work on the bear. The fish biologist was given the syringe and instructions on how to get blood out of a 250-pound bear. Shouldn't be too difficult for a trained biologist who takes blood from three-inch fish. Not quite that easy, as the fish biologist was about to find out.

The professor had handwritten pages of instructions from Bill for the proper procedures, so reading the instructions slowed the work considerably. After a while I eased up alongside the professor and tentatively began to help by handing him the various tools to install the radio collar and ear tags. He seemed to relax and accept the help, so I held the radio collar in place as the professor bolted it on.

Out of the corner of my eye, I was watching the fish biologist who was plunging the big needle over and over into the tender groin area of the poor bear. Every plunge was a dry hole. I don't know how many times he pierced that old bear, but I wouldn't have wanted to be around when that bear woke up. He was probably in a painful condition and a bad humor. Not only had he been poked in the groin numerous times with a large needle, he also had his ears sliced open and two big orange ear tags inserted, a tooth pulled, a paw and leg that were tender from being captured in a cable snare and a big clumsy collar hanging around his neck. No, I would not have wanted to meet that old boy coming down a tight trail the next day. It probably took him a least a week to get back to his normal good-natured black bear humor.

Daryl Adams continued filming so as to catch the gusher of blood when the big needle struck home, but it wasn't happening for the fish biologist. It was easy to see that he was getting frustrated. Finally, after numerous tries with no blood to show for his efforts, the young biologist gave up. He simply stood up, handed me the syringe and said, "You do it."

I took the needle and traded places with the biologist and fully expected to have the same experience as he. Sometimes the bears just didn't want to give up any of their blood to an amateur, and I had had similar experiences in my very short career as a bear biologist helper. I took the syringe, pressed my finger into the groin to find the vein and slipped the needle into the soft flesh. Blood immediately boiled up into the syringe and several little containers were quickly filled.

I must admit that I felt great satisfaction in my success, even though I was a little sorry for the fish biologist who found out it wasn't as easy as it sounded to get blood out of a bear.

In later years I crossed paths with Dr. Bruce Coblentz on numerous occasions and found him to be friendly and amiable. Over the years as I learned more about the Dr. Coblentz, I certainly came to admire and appreciate his abilities and many accomplishments.

The study plan called for ten bears to be captured and collared in the two separate study areas. Shortly after Dr. Coblentz collared the bear, I captured number nine and was looking forward to catching my last bear and pulling snares so that I didn't have to work seven days a week. Bill and I occasionally checked snares for the other guy so we could get a little time off.

After my ninth bear was captured, I went to several new areas of freshly peeled trees and set up six more snares. These were hot sets, and I calculated that I would finish up with my tenth bear in a matter of days. I could then move up to the Valsetz area to do some damage control work and get away from this study and the researcher that I just couldn't seem to get along with. Despite my bad feeling toward Bill, I had planned to spend a day or two getting snares set for him in his area and give him a boost on a few bears from his part of the research area.

I needed a day off, so shortly after setting up the new snares I took Saturday off and Bill ran all my snares that day. When I returned to check snares on Sunday, I found that all my new snare sets had been pulled and I was furious. I was already working past my contract time for OSU and decided that I was done with this partnership. I went out and pulled all the rest of my snares and left Bill to his own devices.

I had had the opportunity for new experiences and learned a lot, but it was time for me to move on. I went north to the Blackrock and Valsetz areas to work on bear damage and captured another half dozen bears before the peeling season ended about the first of July. In all fairness to Bill I expect he could write a story that would be the mirror image of my remembrances.

Ike and the Howling Bears

Ray Aires was managing the Georgia Pacific timberlands in the Alsea drainage west of Corvallis. Georgia Pacific was not a part of our original cooperative, and from what I had heard at that time, not much money was being spent on management of these timberlands. I had also heard that Ray was extremely frugal and I think no one that I was aware of figured that this company would become a part of the bear damage cooperative.

In 1987, a big tour was set up to view some of the bear damage in the Coast Range, and I located several areas of fresh peeling to show people during the tour. A helicopter was brought in, and officials from the Bureau of Land Management (BLM), U.S. Forest Service, Oregon State Forestry, OSU, wildlife biologists and several private company foresters attended the tour. By design the helicopter tour happened to take in a piece of Georgia Pacific land that was experiencing extreme bear damage.

A short time after the tour, Ray had taken his own aerial tour of this area and I presume realized the extent of bear damage in his management area. I soon received a call from Ray which was my first ever conversation with him. He got right to the point, told me to hire someone to take care of that damage and "not to spare the money." It was in this conversation that Ray informed me that Georgia Pacific had contacted Bob Ike about the possibility of doing some bear damage control work and they thought he would be a good choice for the damage control specialist on their lands. This conversation was my first clue that Georgia Pacific was planning on joining the Animal Damage Cooperative.

Bob Ike was an excellent fur and damage control trapper and was the first trapper that I hired as my bear damage control business began to grow. Bob would have preferred working directly for Georgia Pacific, but as it turned out I had the business advantage of already working for a cooperative group of companies. With political safety in numbers, Georgia Pacific decided to join the cooperative and I got the contract. If this call had been made on trapping ability alone, I believe Bob Ike would have gotten the contracting job with Georgia Pacific. I called Bob and talked him into working for me, even though I think he never did like the idea of working for someone else. Over the years I have found this to be a trait of many independent-minded, highly experienced trappers.

Bob was known to me mostly as a highly skilled cat and coyote trapper, but he was also one the few trappers around that had done some bear snaring. Like almost everyone else who knew anything about bear snaring, including myself, he had received his initial training in bears from USDA APHIS. We were about the same age and had both been longline fur trappers during the 1970s and early 1980s.

Bob caught our first bear by just using lure without any bait at the set. It was a wise old female that the local government trapper had been after for some time and had been unable to catch. This bear refused all baits and was the first trap-wise bear we had encountered. Before Bob caught this bear it gave us plenty of evidence of how smart a bear can get given certain circumstances. In later years I developed a very successful line of bear lures, and many tree peelers have fallen to that mysterious odor. Bob also proved that deer could be easily captured in foot snares, and after releasing several we were forced to develop ways of not catching the numerous blacktail deer in those snares.

In my third year of contracting, I turned over the snaring responsibilities in the Alsea country to Bob and I moved north into the Black Rock and Valsetz areas. One day when I was working seventy-five air miles north of Bob's area, he called me on our high-powered radio phone. These phones were on an open line and could be listened to by numerous unknown people, so we couldn't talk freely about bears. Bob only let me know that he had some problem and needed help as soon as I could get there.

It took me over three hours to get to where he wanted to meet me. I pulled out on an old logging landing on the head of Bull Run Creek and stepped out to meet him. He informed me that he had a bear drag and snare missing from his set and the drag marks disappeared over the edge and down into the canyon. The fact that the snare was missing wasn't the problem. The problem was that the big canyon below us sounded like it was full of bears! Grunts, growls, bellowing, groans and a whining that sounded curiously like a dirt bike winding up in the distance were echoing all over the canyon.

It was clear that Bob had no desire to go into that canyon alone, and by the howls that reverberated from the devil's club thickets below, I had plenty of sympathy for that line of thinking. Nevertheless, we had to complete the job, and with safety in numbers, we started to follow up the drag trail and find our bear. Together we dropped over the steep canyon wall, I with my 06 Auto, and Ike, pistol in hand, over the edge fifty yards to my right. One hundred yards down the brush-filled cow's face, I saw the vine maple tops jerking and swaying as a good-sized bear stuck its head up over a windfall log and was obviously caught in the snare.

Just as I was starting to take aim, I heard a scratching to my left and saw a bear coming down a hundred-foot-tall fir tree that had recently been peeled. I aimed and fired, dropping the bear out of the tree, and turned back to the bear in front of me. I quickly dispatched that bear and had not yet moved, when again the noise started to my left and another bear was coming down out of a tall fir at a fast pace. I fired quickly and had the third bear within less than a minute. It didn't take long to realize this was a sow with two half-grown yearlings, and they had peeled dozens of tall forty-five-year-old Douglas fir trees.

There is no "thrill of the chase" in this type of bear hunting. The object of damage control hunting is to remove the bears that are the worst offenders at peeling trees, no matter which bear or bears it may be. By selectively taking the individuals that are destroying valuable crop trees, the control program focuses on individuals as opposed to the general bear population.

Over the years since this incident, I have occasionally heard the buzz-saw or dirt-bike-like noise coming from a snared bear in the distance, but never since the day Bob Ike and I tracked down the howling bears have I heard such a variety of noises echoing around a Coast Range canyon.

Scott Takes a Turkey

I had known Scott Lafond ever since he and his brother, Allen, had shown me how to trap boomers in 1979. The Lafond Family eventually got out of the contract trapping business, and in 1989 I hired Scott on a spring bear-snaring job. Scott was well qualified as he was an experienced hunter and trapper and had the additional value of knowing the Alsea country better than I did. Scott was easy to get along with and we both shared a love of hunting.

Turkeys were a big thing about this time and flocks were popping up all over the Oregon Coast Range. Neither Scott nor I knew much about turkey hunting but had been steeping ourselves in the minute details of every turkey hunting article we could find. Every time we rode together on the bear trapline we would discuss turkey hunting and both agreed that from what we had read, that it must be nearly impossible for the neophyte hunter to bag one.

Scott was setting bear snares on a piece of Starker Forest property called Aire King, and we both knew that turkeys had been seen in the area, but as yet we hadn't had a visual on them. One day Scott was using the ATV to haul bear bait back to a snare location, when suddenly a big tom turkey appeared on the dirt track some one hundred yards up the road from him. Scott eased the ATV to a stop and knelt down in the road to watch. The big tom was strutting around and gobbling, and Scott was in awe of this most majestic big bird reportedly so difficult to hunt. After a few minutes, Scott decided to get a little closer, so he crouched down and began a slow forward stalk up the old logging skid trail. Closer and closer he moved, as the big tom continued to strut and then began moving down the road toward Scott.

What luck! Scott was beside himself with excitement. Holding his breath and trying to stay calm, Scott continued to close the distance until he and the turkey were only a few yards apart. At this point Scott began to wonder why this wisest of all birds hadn't made a quick dash to nearby cover. The bird now seemed to be looking him right in the eye.

Deciding that he was close enough, Scott stood straight up intending to flush the bird. Instead of running away, the big tom darted right at Scott who turned in surprise and ran back down the trail. Thinking that he would outdistance the bird easily, after a few yards he slowed and turned around only to find the turkey closing in fast.

Now, truly frightened, Scott sprinted with renewed vigor. Sighting a good stick, he scooped it up and turned to face his attacker. The big tom launched up and attempted to use his spurs. Jumping aside, with a quick whack Scott turned the wild turkey into dead meat with a broken neck.

I, of course, knew nothing of this turkey hunt until long after the fact, although much later I did find a strange bagful of feathers at our bear snare location. In later discussions, Scott and I both decided that the intelligence of wild turkeys was somewhat overrated.

In the Christmas Spirit

By 1989, I had been doing bear control work in the upper Siletz drainage for three years and had become very familiar with much of that rugged coastal mountain area. While doing spring bear control I had noted a great deal of bobcat sign and decided to run a trapline that winter. As usual I started trapping cats and beaver about the first of December. At the time, most of this country was owned by Willamette Industries, Georgia Pacific, Boise Cascade, and the Bureau of Land Management. Much of the lands had been logged with railroads during the early 1900s and had grown back into second growth timber with plenty of brush lands.

This is fairly remote country with hundreds of square miles of nothing but timberlands and no habitations. Many days I would run my traplines all day without seeing even one other vehicle on these old logging road systems. I was trapping out of my home in Albany at the time and the line would usually run about 250 miles per day. I normally arrived home about nine o'clock in the evening.

Long after dark in late December, I was coming out of the Blackrock area about twenty miles from the nearest civilization on the high ridges above the little company town of Valsetz. It was a typical Coast Range winter day of strong southwest winds and heavy rain. I stopped after checking my last trap and pulled off my rain gear and pistol, shoving them back up under the seat and out of the way. I turned the defroster and heater up on high and rolled the window down to try to de-fog the windows in my small truck. It was then pedal to the metal down the pitch-black night with the pouring rain and a light fog settling in.

The headlights cut a dim path in the dark night as I sped out the snakelike gravel road system toward the little town of Fall City. Fifteen miles from pavement I rounded a sharp corner in the road and was suddenly confronted with a young lady running down the road toward my truck.

Blood streamed down her distorted face, and although I couldn't hear her, it was obvious she was screaming in sheer terror. I slid to a stop somewhat sideways in the road as she grabbed for my door handle and started jerking on it, all the while screaming incoherently.

Having earlier rested my arm on the door frame I had unknowingly depressed the lock on my door, and this terrified girl couldn't gain entry. I sat there stunned for a moment trying to figure out what to do. I couldn't see to back up, my gun was stuffed up under the seat and out of reach. A pickup truck was overturned in the ditch twenty yards in front of my truck. The terrified girl and the overturned truck were not all that had stunned me. In the middle of the road fifteen yards from my truck stood a man with a long barreled, large caliber pistol. He was waving the gun around wildly and looking straight at my truck.

The young lady appeared to be about twenty years old. She suddenly ran around my pickup and jumped in through the passenger side door, slid across the seat and up tightly against me, still screaming at the top of her lungs but not making any sense. I paid little attention to her but watched as the young disheveled man slowly walked up to my window still waving the big pistol around.

"This is it," I thought. "He is going to shoot me and I have nowhere to go."

He walked up to my window holding the gun in front of him, apparently very drunk. I sat in silence as he said, "Get out of the pickup and I'll show you what happened here."

"Oh no," I said, in my friendliest voice. "Why don't you jump in the pickup and I'll take you out and get some help."

He repeated his words and I then repeated mine. We then each repeated those same words several times. It was still not clear to me what was going on, when suddenly the young man smiled, lifted the gun up to my window and said, "Here, take this, it's unloaded." I nearly passed out, having just thought he was going to shoot me.

The young man went around and got in the truck, and the two of them suddenly became very happy and started giggling. They were both very drunk and began to jabber. It turned out they were brother and sister on an outing to get a Christmas tree and had certainly brought plenty of spirits with them.

I cleaned some of the blood off the girl's face and the terrified look was replaced with pure joy at having been saved. She kissed me on the cheek and began profusely thanking me for saving her life. The conversation was pretty much repetitive as we drove along, but I soon found out what had so terrified the girl.

First, she had just wrecked her second pickup in a month, both of which had belonged to another brother. Secondly, as her brother told in great detail and drunken delight, the moment before I had arrived she had been lying face down in the muddy gravel road pounding her fists and screaming that the "bears were going to eat her." It never entered my mind that she was running to me to be saved from the bears!

Draggin' Beaver

Late spring of 1990 found me again in the rugged Siletz drainage of the Oregon Coast Range working hard at finding fresh bear peeling. There was extensive bear damage in the big second growth timber of the jumbled canyons and ridges for several miles around where the North Fork of the Siletz and Boulder Creek came together. A big patch of huge old growth timber had been preserved up the North Fork at a place called The Valley of the Giants. This preserve is well worth seeing and I often took visitors on my trapline for a quick look at some of the huge old growth trees in this stand. The nearby old growth with vast stands of big second growth and the roadless, inaccessible canyons made ideal bear habitat.

High on the ridge above the North Fork of the Siletz and just south of the mouth of Boulder Creek, an old unused logging road had been carved into the side of a steep mountain. This road had not been used for years and in many places brush, trees and boulders restricted it to a one-lane trail. I had previously walked out this old logging road and found several scattered fresh peeled trees along its one-mile length with several freshly peeled trees on the old log landing at the very end of the road. I thought this would make an ideal bear snare location.

The road was too overgrown for an ATV. On closer inspection, I realized that with a minimal amount of power saw work and an hour or so with a pick and shovel, I would be able to ride my three-wheeled Kawasaki to the end of the road and quickly retrieve any bears that I caught. On several occasions I'd had to pack bears out on my back, and it made life much easier to drag them out with mechanical help when possible. The first quarter mile of the road to a washout or slide was pretty open, and I was able with very little effort to get that far with the cycle.

With pick and shovel I set to work to dig a four-foot-wide trail across the twelve-foot gap in the road, and two hours later had a fairly serviceable trail down into the slide and up the far side on a trail that leaned a little toward the downhill or canyon side of the trail. Truthfully, it looked a little scary for motorized use since the mountainside dropped dramatically off into the canyon below.

I took a deep breath and drove over the edge and up the steep sideling trail to flat ground on the far side of the washout. A little euphoric sense of accomplishment hit me, and immediately I ran the ATV back and forth across the slide several times to pack the loose dirt and get the feel of negotiating the scary little dip. I then headed on out the old roadbed cutting open the trail as I went to allow the ATV to navigate the trail. In another two hours, I had the overgrown trail brushed out to the end and had arrived on the secluded landing in the prime bear snare location.

Dropping my gear there, I zoomed back out the trail, and in just a few minutes had traversed the new pack trail out over the washout and back to my truck for my snare, bait and other equipment to put in a bear set.

A somewhat ripe beaver for bait resided in the back of my truck, so instead of loading the smelly thing on the back rack I decided to tow it behind the ATV with about eight feet of rope. I surmised that the scent trail leading to the end of the old road might just get a bear to head that direction and get tangled up in my snare. After attaching the roped carcass to the back rack of the ATV I loaded additional supplies on the rack and set off down the trail at a good clip with Mr. Beaver bouncing along behind.

I soon arrived at the washout, and with the confidence of several trips across the slide I dropped over the edge and throttled a little power to pull me up the steep incline on the far side. As I hit the bottom of my new trail, the forty-pound beaver snapped over the edge of the drop-off as if on a rubber band and quickly rolled to the downhill side of my little trail and over the edge. As I started up the steep part of the trail toward flat ground, the beaver on a rope rolled directly downhill from me, and the ATV acted as if I had thrown an anchor overboard into eight feet of water.

The light front end of the three-wheeled ATV went up in the air and the rear end was jerked sideways at the same time. I was ejected backwards off the tricycle and flew down the washout landing upside down about ten feet from the trail.

I landed on my shoulders and head in the sandstone rocks and rubble with the ATV flying in midair over the top of me. My feet were straight in the air, and as the rig came over I was able to push it off with both feet. It had gained speed so quickly that the small force of my kick lifted it just above my upsidedown head, and it missed me completely as it crashed into the rocks and rolled end over end before coming to rest against a small log lodged sideways in the steep washout. That log was the last object in the washout slide for four hundred yards with my ATV lodged perilously against it.

I was momentarily stunned and saw stars for a few moments before I regained my senses. I did a slow back summersault to my knees and expected the worst as I kneeled there trying to regain my composure.

I slowly gained my feet and was amazed that other than my

bruised noggin and a few scrapes, all other body parts seemed to be working. I couldn't even find any blood which was a little disappointing since it seemed I had narrowly escaped from what should have been a very serious injury or fatal accident. It was hard to believe that the three-hundred-pound airborne ATV had not smashed my head into the rocks as it came hurtling over me. I crawled up the washout and onto the trail, sitting there for several minutes with my head still spinning and my body starting to hurt in several places.

I eyed my upsidedown ATV for a few minutes but eventually decided I needed to get up and move, so I started back out the trail and headed for my truck. A little walking loosened me up, and with only an aching head and some deep bruises I fairly quickly traversed the trail back to my truck. Grabbing the power saw winch I usually used to drag bears up out of the rugged mountainsides, I headed back out the trail with the awkward fifty-pound machine.

Arriving at the accident site, I cabled the winch to a handy tree on the upside of the trail and unraveled the winch line down the mountain thirty yards to the cycle and hooked it up. I then fired up the saw and began to slowly winch the rig up over the steep incline. Twenty minutes later, I had my ATV back on flat ground in an upright position. Amazingly I could find nothing broken and the faithful old machine fired right up.

Loading my gear, I headed back to my truck and decided that was enough bear trapping for one day. I felt very lucky to still have my ATV and even luckier to have not been seriously hurt. I got to thinking that bear trapping was a somewhat dangerous business, but unlike what many people might think, that danger often had very little to do with bears. It seemed like most of the danger was always in the coming and going to the bear hunting grounds.

Cougar Attack by Sharon Davis

The Big Cats

Call them cougars, mountain lions, lions, puma, panthers, cata-
mount, painter or kitties. Whatever you might call one of these big
cats, when you see one up close and personal it will bring some
excitement into your day. I can say with certainty that in my years
of bear control work and trapping I have had all the lion excitement
I wanted, and then some.

The big toms are especially menacing, and I have never looked
into a more fearful set of eyes than a large tom cougar that intended
to kill and eat me. Today in Oregon, hundreds of deer see that look
of murder just before they take their last breath on earth, and I suspect there are not many living creatures that have seen that look and
lived for more than a few minutes. I did see that look and will tell
you what it was like!

On March 6, 1843, at the home of the old Hudson's Bay trapper Joseph Gervais, the Oregon provincial government enacted a
bounty on cougars. "Wolf meetings" had been held to discuss how
to solve the problem of increasing attacks on local livestock by
wolves, bears and cougars. At the March 6 meeting, a bounty system
was developed calling for settlers to contribute to a general fund that
would pay bounties to hunters who killed predators. An executive
committee was selected and the first local tax enacted.

Historians today often make light of the bounty portion of these
first meetings of the early Oregon government, but my bet is that
predators were first on the list of important steps for the settlers
to take, and government was a distant second. Eventually, through
many years of bounties, the predator problem was brought mostly

but never completely under control.

By the 1960s, many thought cougar populations in Oregon were low. At that time cougar caused relatively few problems with livestock, at least compared to past history. In 1967, Oregon reclassified the mountain lion or cougar as a big game animal, and then in 1994, Oregon voters passed Measure 18 banning hounds, the most effective tool for hunting cougars. Over the next fifteen years the cougar population steadily increased.

By the late 1990s, cougars were commonly observed by outdoorsmen, and livestock depredation had become quite common, even in the more populated Willamette Valley. By the early 2000s, the cougar population was at a level not seen for decades. Foresters, hunters, outdoorsmen, rural residents and even suburban residents were sighting cougars, even in some highly populated areas.

It is a real adrenalin rush to see a mountain lion close up, and they have always been one of the more exciting elements of the bear damage control business. Cougars were rarely our target animal, but since they lived in the same habitat as the bears we were attempting to catch, and cougar populations were high, we usually managed to snag a couple or more of them each season.

It is definitely exciting to see such a large dangerous predator up close when captured in a foot snare, but the most thrilling moments always came when it was time to release them. Oregon law classifies mountain lions as big game, and as such they can only be taken with a big game tag during an established season, when they are doing some kind of depredation, or when they are a danger or health risk to the public. Since the cougars that we captured were usually not doing damage, we were required by the Oregon Department of Fish and Wildlife to turn them loose.

During the mid-1990s, my bear damage control contracts covered a large part of western Oregon. We were working from the northern Lane County Cascades east of Springfield and from Triangle Lake to the very northwest corner of the state at Astoria in the Coast Range mountains. Altogether at that time, I had under contract somewhere around a million acres to oversee for bear damage control. This included numerous private timber company lands along with the Tillamook and Clatsop state forests. While all these regions held good cougar populations, the Cascades in Lane County was definitely the hot spot for catching lions. Paul Carlisle worked for me in this area, and I would fairly frequently receive a call from him or from one of the other snare men that we had a cougar to release.

Most of the time when Paul called, I would be setting or checking snares about seventy-five to a hundred miles north and west of his damage area, so we often ended up releasing lions in the late evening long after dark. Paul would find a cougar in one of his snares at some point during the day and give me a call. We would both finish up our day of checking bear snares and then meet as quickly as I could get down to his area. I later became certified to use a tranquilizer gun for releasing non-target catches, but in the earlier years of bear damage control we didn't have that option.

My first question to Paul was always, "How big is it?" If Paul indicated that it was a big mature tom, we would contact the Oregon Department of Fish and Wildlife and get them to come out and chemically immobilize the critter. ODFW biologists were very helpful over the years but this was always our last choice. It seemed to take forever to get anyone from the department on the phone and even harder to get them out to a remote area to release a cougar in a timely manner.

If the cat was approaching a hundred pounds or more, however, I just wasn't brave enough to tackle them with my six-foot dog catcher pole. Over the years, we got home at 2:00 a.m. on several occasions after releasing a lion. Once certification for chemical immobilization was accomplished, it speeded up the release of each cougar by several hours, and I am sure the big cats appreciated it.

More often than not, Paul would indicate that he thought we could handle the cougar ourselves, and we soon worked out an efficient method for releasing cougars up to about one hundred pounds. I had a six-foot dog catcher pole, or as we called it, a choke pole. I would slip up on one side of the trapped cougar and Paul would come up on the opposite side. The snare which held the cougar was attached to a tree by about eight feet of 3/16-inch airplane cable, and this allowed for a sixteen-foot circle for the cat to run around in and avoid being snared with the choke pole. Most lions don't really want a noose around their neck and will often grab the cable noose in their teeth and hold on. The only way to get the big cat to let go is to move in close so that he thinks he might get a chance at biting the snare man.

Often the only way to corner the cougar is to get inside the catch circle with it, and that always adds an element of excitement. Usually after a few minutes of stalk and jump, I could get the noose around the neck of the lion and try to choke the air out of him. I remember the game I played as a kid of trying to hold my breath long enough to pass out. Of course, this is not a smart thing to do, but then I was never famous for being a smart kid. At any rate, the process is similar for releasing a cougar from a trap or foot snare. The plan is to choke the animal just long enough for it to pass out, quickly release it from the snare, then stand back to see what happens. Over the years I have successfully released many bobcats and cougars seemingly unharmed by this method.

I remember one good-sized tom cougar that Paul Carlisle caught up in the Gate Creek country of the McKenzie River drainage. Paul called me early one afternoon with the news that he had captured a cougar in one of his bear snares. According to Paul, it was on the big side, but he thought we could accomplish the release without the help of the Oregon Department of Fish and Wildlife. Scott Lafond, one of the bear trappers, wanted to see a cougar release so I rounded him up and we headed up the McKenzie to meet Paul.

We arrived in the daylight which is always a plus. Maybe it's just me, but bears and cougars seem to be much more aggressive in the dark, and I definitely feel more comfortable releasing a cougar in the daylight. This tom appeared to be approaching one hundred pounds and was about as big as I wanted to handle.

After the usual sparing match, I was finally able to get the snare pole loop around the cougar's neck and set the hook. The loose end of the snare loop runs back through the snare pole, and when this tag end is pulled, it tightens up the loop. I would wrap this loose cable end around my leather gloved hand and pull with all my strength to choke the animal down. The result of that action is somewhere between setting the hook on a large Chinook salmon and turning a bucking bronco out of the rodeo chute. It is necessary to hang on tight or the cougar will end up with a necklace that you can't control.

As usual this cougar went up on its hind legs and then began to twist and roll to escape the noose. After a short time the cougar went down on its side, and although breathing hard he would not pass out. After several minutes the cougar seemed no worse for wear despite my best efforts to choke him and just continued to breathe hard and stare right through me.

Finally in desperation, I had Paul cut the snare loose from the tree it was tied to. Paul was able to slip in and use our cable cutters to snip the three-sixteenth-inch airplane cable, and the cougar was now free except for the dog choke pole around his neck and a foot snare with eight feet of attached cable dangling from his leg. Suddenly the catch pole seemed like very little protection and I quickly maneuvered a tree between me and the cougar. It then occurred to me that it wasn't such a good idea to cut the snare cable, but now there was no turning back.

I redoubled my effort to choke the air out of this cougar but the snare pole was in the wrong position on his neck and nothing I could do would have any effect. After a few more minutes of this effort I began to feel both my arms become numb from straining. It was clear this cougar was not in any way impaired by my efforts to subdue him and I wouldn't be able to hold on much longer. I could envision a cougar running off through the woods with my snare and eight feet of airplane cable trailing behind and a six-foot dog catcher pole tightly secured around his neck. I knew it was now or never to get the snare off its foot.

I quickly circled part way around the tree so that the cougar was on one side and its paw with attached cable was on the other. Paul gingerly moved into position only inches away from the other lethal pie-plate-sized paw, and after some effort he was able to snip the snare completely off the tom's foot with the cable cutters.

Finally, we had the big cat completely free from the snare, and the only thing left to do was to release the spring-loaded neck loop. Paul and Scott moved back a few yards and Scott held my pistol at the ready for protection, which honestly didn't give me much comfort. I could easily visualize myself getting cut to ribbons by a mad tom cougar while at the same time being shot with my own .44 Magnum.

Nevertheless, when Scott and Paul were stationed and ready, I released the spring catch and removed the noose. The tom continued to lie on its side for a moment and then rolled over and sat on its haunches just like a dog! I stood frozen less than five feet from where the cougar sat looking directly at me for maybe three or four seconds.

It was a long few seconds, but with that beautiful fluid movement that all cougars seem to have, he just turned, rolled sideways and melted away into the dense underbrush. I will never forget the look on that cougar's face. It was slightly puzzled, much as if to say, "Why did you do that?"

Fortunately, all the cougars we released over the years decided the best thing to do was to exit the area. It seems to me that the only time you need to worry about a cougar is when they have it in head to procure something to eat. They rarely fail or change their mind when they start down that path. Eating and fighting are two different subjects, and given the chance to flee a confrontation the lion in my experience always takes that path.

Another big tom cougar that I ran into definitely had dinner on his mind, and the fearsome look on his face and in his eyes quickly established this event as the most terrifying few moments of my life. It was in early March 2000, and I had decided to get away to the southeastern Oregon desert for a few days of bushman's holiday, hunting antlers and maybe doing a little fishing before I got wrapped up in another season of bear damage control work.

I went down to Lakeview and then on to Adel for a last fuel stop before traveling another fifty miles and setting up camp near a beautiful desert spring that Indians had used previously as a camp-ground for thousands of years. Broken bits of obsidian arrowheads littered the ground around the spring and petroglyphs dotted many rock walls in the area.

My old trapper friend, Woody Merrill, had told me about this spot. He had hunted and trapped the area for many years. Woody's stories of big mule deer bucks of the 1940s and '50s were what had drawn me to this spot, and I had in mind to hunt antlers in some rugged country to the south and down near the Nevada state line.

Early morning found me up and hiking south toward Nevada through an open rocky plateau. There was a beautiful little isolated desert stream and lots of junipers in a little valley to the west of me, but the plateau was wide open grassland with rocky outcroppings, a few big rimrocks and small patches of sagebrush in a few spots.

This area was completely new to me, and since I didn't know where the deer were located it was pretty much a shot in the dark as far as horn hunting. Not that I really cared since I wasn't a real horn

Charlie Mock at a petroglyph rock near my horn hunting camp.

hunter. I was just using this as an excuse for seeing some new country and, as always, keeping an eye out for cat and coyote sign just
in case I might want to do a little trapping in the area at some point.

By 9:00 a.m. I had hiked several miles from camp and was in
a pretty remote area. The surrounding country has lots of two-track
desert trails, but I had located an area with very rough vehicle access
and consequently few people traveled the area, especially at this
time of year. There is not much to fear in these remote desert areas,
but the weight of my new Colt stainless target model pistol still felt
good as it rode comfortably in my shoulder holster under my warm
camo jacket. I never worry much about wild animals in these areas,
however, several surprise encounters with some strange people in
remote areas over the years is reason enough to carry some self-
protection when alone in remote areas.

There is also the survival factor if something goes wrong and you need something to eat. This day would eventually prove to me how useless the handgun would be, stored in a deeply covered shoulder holster, if I ever did need it for protection from a wild animal attack.

After a lot of hiking, I finally discovered some old deer tracks and was encouraged that I might eventually find a horn or two somewhere in this vast landscape. I traveled along a nice rimrock about thirty feet high on my right, and on my left was one of the infrequent patches of sagebrush that was about thigh high. Between the rimrock and the sagebrush was an open area of about six feet with a good game trail leading along the rimrock.

My head was down and my eyes were searching for what often looks like a white stick when first observed but might turn out to be the single tine of a large desert buck's shed antler. I was headed south on the game trail and on my east side the sage patch ran for approximately sixty feet.

Suddenly, in the sagebrush to my left, I heard the unmistakable sound of a large deer busting out of its bed to depart the area. Having heard the commotions of a deer leaving its bed on many occasions in my fifty-plus years of hunting experience, there was no question about what I had heard. Or so I thought.

As I lifted my head to watch the deer bounding away I was shocked to see not a deer's rear end departing but instead the head, shoulders and forelegs of a huge tom cougar just rising up above the sagebrush with his eyes locked on me at a distance of about twenty-five feet. The lion was just starting to launch his second jump which could easily reach me where I stood frozen in my tracks.

The lion's front feet were off the ground and the final energy just being delivered to his powerful spring-loaded hind legs when our eyes met. Never in my life have I seen such a look of murder written on the face of any animal. This cougar had a kill within easy reach

This big cat made it quite clear who's the boss.

and was just two seconds from burying claws and fangs. The look said he could already taste blood, and it never changed when he realized that I was not a deer but a human. He simply rolled sideways in that beautiful fluid movement that big cats are capable of and, in two bounds, was out of sight behind a four-foot-high rock outcropping that petered out into a rolling rock-covered hillside. I never saw him again, even though it looked as if I could see every blade of grass beyond the end of the little rock outcropping.

Unlike other close calls that I have had over the years, this one shook me to the core. The look on that cougar's face just wouldn't go away, and in the split second that our eyes met, I knew that he had me. There was nothing I could do. It was lucky for me this killing machine checked his charge at the last second. This event proved again for me that it is a short distance between life and death.

I madly worked at trying to quick draw my pistol, but by the time I retrieved it from under my jacket, the cougar was long gone. It was easy enough to figure out later from the tracks and sign that the lion was crouching in the sage and watching my legs as I got closer and closer to him. I am sure he thought all along that I was a deer and his dinner was about to be served.

For the next two hours, I carried the pistol in my hand with the safety off until very slowly my fear passed into an uncomfortable memory. I can still easily recall that big cat as he started that final leap. The look in those eyes, the broad chest, and those rippling muscular forelegs were an awesome sight. Cougar are the most lethal killer that resides in our neck of the woods. It is a good thing that most of the time they choose not to put us clumsy humans on the menu.

Axe Handles and Ex-Cons

Things were just not working out for my desert bobcat trapping adventure in January of 2005. My longtime hunting and trapping partner, Charlie Mock, and I had been planning since the previous year when we had trapped the high desert of eastern Oregon to return to the same area this year. The best laid plans don't always work out, and Charlie was having serious problems with his bee business and cancelled out only a couple of weeks before we were to leave.

Then the weather turned ferocious, and snow storm after snow storm hit the high desert area that we had planned to trap. The main highway that I needed to travel was closed completely for several days. It was now out of the question to pull my little travel trailer into the snowbound remote desert area that I had wanted to trap.

With the weather so bad and Charlie bailing on me, I had to make some quick decisions. With traps, equipment and an ATV, I had no way of towing a travel trailer or room to pack a camping outfit. I also had to deal with my wife who wasn't very excited about my traipsing off to such a remote area for three weeks of trapping alone. Compromise was in order. I had no intention of canceling the trip and soon decided a less remote and "safer" trapline area would have to do.

Three years before, I had rented a small cabin at Valley Falls. The owners of this small oasis thirty miles north of Lakeview were friendly and the accommodations were great for a trapper. Jim and Joann owned a combination service station, restaurant, store and local meeting place. They had a duplex rental cabin that was probably built in the 1930s or early '40s. The attached cabins weren't fancy but were just what I needed. They were each self-contained with a small kitchen, a bed, shower and electric heat. All I needed was a sleeping bag and some food. The stove, refrigerator and cooking utensils were included.

Jim and Joann had rented the cabin to me by the week and the total price ended up amounting to seven dollars per night, a price that would have been hard to argue with in 1950! The cabins were joined by a thin wall, but no one else was staying on the other side and the place had been quiet and peaceful in 2002. After Charlie cancelled on me I quickly decided to trap in this more secure area, even though the area was overrun with trappers and the competition would be stiff. I would call Jim and Joann to see if I could again rent one of the little self-contained cabins.

Joann answered the phone call but was very hesitant to rent the cabin to me. Someone was staying in the cabin I had rented before and the other cabin had some problems. The shower didn't work quite right and the place needed a good cleaning. I told Joann that I would fix the plumbing and clean the place myself. She came up with several more excuses, but I finally prevailed and she agreed with much hesitation to rent the cabin to me. I was quite relieved when she finally relented, even though the price had moved up to the incredible amount of ten dollars per day.

A few days later, I had my vehicle loaded to the brim with the trapping equipment I would need for three weeks of high desert trapping. Early on Thursday morning I departed the wet, dark and gloomy west side of Oregon for the clear skies and cold air of the eastern side of the state. The farther I got from home the greater my anticipation of the coming trapline.

The area I was headed for is cowboy country with a rich history, where cowboy hats and boots are working attire for many and where cows are likely to be pushed right down the main highway or the main street of any small community. I shoved a CD into the player and listened to cowboy songs over and over. No one was with me to complain about the repetition and I never grow tired of hearing Marty Robbins ballads. One of my all-time favorite songs is "Strawberry Roan," and I played it over and over. After long hours on the road, I rolled into Valley Falls just before dark. A lone streetlight hung over the country store and dimly illuminated the little duplex cabin.

Jim was just closing up the store as I arrived. He was a cowboy through and through, eighty years old or thereabouts and still breaking horses. He was tall, thin and raw boned, with a permanent cowboy hat and a neckerchief around his neck, soft-spoken but not a man to be trifled with. After shaking hands and renewing our acquaintance, I started to depart the store to unload my gear into the cabin. As I walked out the door, Jim added to our short conversation. "By the way, if that guy in the other cabin gives you any trouble, just let me know. I'll take care of it. He's mean when he's drunk and he's schizophrenic. He just got out of jail but usually he just stays in the cabin and lifts weights all day."

"Great," I thought. "A crazy, drunk outlaw is in the adjoining cabin." I calmly answered, "Not to worry, I can get along with almost anyone."

The stars were brilliant and the moon reflected a soft glow off the white frozen landscape as I walked across the gravel road to the cabin. My mind drifted back to an earlier time when I had first set eyes on Valley Falls. It was 1956 and I was six years old. It was my first hunting trip to eastern Oregon and my first time to experience that cold clear air and the smell of sage brush and pine. Of course, I didn't actually hunt but was just along for the camping trip.

Valley Falls is a unique place, located just a mile or so west of Abert Rim, named by John C. Freemont in 1843. Abert Rim is one of the largest, longest, exposed fault escarpments in North America and rises some 2,500 feet above the desert floor. The view was spectacular to a young boy, but the baboon and rattlesnake in the cages out front, the numerous arrowhead collections on the inside walls, and the dozen or so giant mule deer head mounts were unforgettable images that are sharp in my mind, even fifty-plus years later.

As I stepped onto the cabin porch I came back to the present and saw the window curtain pull back in the adjoining cabin as a shadowy figure peeked out. I entered the unlocked door and found the cabin toasty warm. The place was freshly cleaned and the shower had been fixed. I heard no sounds from next door so I quickly unloaded my gear, shut the flimsy old wooden door and rustled up a little grub for supper.

After supper, all was quiet. Jim's worrisome words about my neighbor, whom I began to call Brutus, were beginning to fade, and I began to relax and anticipate a full day ahead of setting traps. I sat down at the small kitchen table with a cup of hot tea and surveyed my surroundings. The walls were covered with a floral print paper from an earlier time with a couple of old cheap pictures hanging askew by nails. The kitchen cabinets were white enameled metal of a past era with rust spots worn through. The bed appeared to be of about vintage 1910 and the springs had probably worn out thirty years ago. I folded up like a suitcase when I lay on it for the first time. After a quick survey I decided the cabin was nearly perfect. The place is warm and dry with a hot shower, stove, refrigerator, electric lights. All in all, far better than most of my trapping camps. I pulled out my journal, filled in the day's activities and rolled myself into bed.

At 4:30 a.m. the next morning I hit the road. A hundred miles later, I left the pavement for thirty more miles of four-wheel-drive mud and snow before reaching the area I wanted to start trapping. My wife wouldn't really need to know how far I was trapping from my secure and safe location.

Several nights later I pulled into Valley Falls long after dark. Inside the cabin I fired up the stove and cooked a big batch of buttermilk pancakes and venison steaks. After a couple of cups of hot tea, I sat down at the table for my normal ritual of filling my journal with the activities of the day.

It was incredibly quiet. Three inches of snow muffled any outside noise, only rarely would a vehicle pass by on the highway and not even a dog could be heard barking. No television, no radio and no close neighbors to make any noise. Just silence. After several days, I had not heard or seen my neighbor, and only a rare thump in the other cabin reminded me that he was there.

Suddenly, BANG, BANG, BANG, BANG! My neighbor seemed to have gone berserk just behind the thin walls of my kitchen area. It sounded like he was hitting the metal cabinets with a stick or his fists or something. The banging on the cabinets was soon followed by cursing and threatening talk, all directed at me. I was told in no uncertain terms to BE QUIET!!! Trouble was, I wasn't making a sound.

In fact, I didn't move a muscle as the banging and yelling continued.

I soon realized that intimidation was his plan, and to be truthful it was working quite well. Finally, fearing imminent attack, I got up and locked the flimsy door and eyed my holstered 22 revolver lying on the counter. I quietly put a pan of water on the stove to heat and sat back down to see what might transpire. Nothing like a pan of scalding water to slow a bully down, I surmised.

The banging stopped, but after a short reprieve it started up again and lasted for another ten minutes, then silence.

During the banging and cursing I was trying to make a plan. My landlord lived about a block away, but running to an eighty-plus-year-old senior citizen for help, even if he was a tough old cowboy, just didn't seem right. The other nearest neighbors were about half a mile away but I didn't know them or anyone else at the ranches thinly scattered around the valley. It seemed like I would just have to handle this on my own.

I turned off the lights inside my cabin and sat quietly for nearly an hour sipping my cup of tea, my pan of water simmering on the hot stove. Nothing happened except silence, and I finally calmed down, slipped over to the bed and held my breath as the rusty old springs screeched as I lay down. I was giving serious thought to moving out of this place, but finally with no more banging I drifted off to sleep. At 4:00 a.m. the next morning I quietly slipped out the door and headed out to check traps.

On January 20, I had a particularly tough day, stuck in the snow for over three hours and traveling over 250 miles without catching a cat. I shuffled into the cabin at 8:00 p.m., fixed a quick bowl of soup and slipped quietly into bed. Just as I was about to drift off, my neighbor started pounding on the wall and beating on the metal cabinets. This lasted about ten minutes and then all was silent. My trapping trowel lay on one side of me and my pistol remained in my hand. Sleep didn't come easily but I finally drifted off. At 4:00 a.m. I was up and quickly departed for the trapline. It felt good to get some distance between me and the bully neighbor whom I had only briefly glimpsed.

The next evening, I came back to the cabin after dark and was expecting the worst. I quickly entered my cabin, locked the door and took care of the evening chores as quietly as possible. My nerves were on edge, but all was quiet and I went to bed and began to relax.

For the next several days I continued to set and check traps, putting in long days and catching only an occasional cat, badger or coyote. The combination of snow, new country and a lack of experience at desert trapping was beating me up pretty good.

On January 25, my old friend Woody Merrill from Lakeview, came up to ride with me for the day and share some much needed instructions on desert cat trapping. Woody had been in this country for over sixty years and had taken hundreds of desert cats. His prime purpose this day was to show me one of his best traplines and help me to catch a few cats.

After a short day, Woody and I came back to my cabin about 3:30 in the afternoon, and for the first time I saw my neighbor. He was a burly character sitting on the steps of his cabin drinking a beer as I drove in. He immediately slipped into his cabin and disappeared. I unloaded my ATV, cleaned up and departed for Lakeview to do some laundry and have a good dinner with Woody. After dinner I headed back for Valley Falls.

I arrived just before dark and pulled up in front of my cabin. Sitting on the steps of his cabin just six feet from my cabin door and twenty feet from my truck was the "friendly" neighbor. The lights were on in Jim's house about a block away but otherwise it appeared that we were the only two people around for miles. I took a deep breath and got out of my truck, immediately going around to the back and hooking up the ramp to load my ATV.

I glanced up and, sure enough, here he came. "Why are you out here trying to hurt those coyotes?" he asked in a grim slurred voice.

"They are my friends." The words in Marty Robbins song "Strawberry Roan" came ringing back into my ears: "I could see with one eye he's a regular outlaw."

This guy was about five-foot-ten, solid muscle with huge biceps. He had several days' growth of black beard and was obviously drunk. His face wore a twisted scowl as he stared directly at me. He was fifteen years my junior and I knew at a glance that in a physical confrontation, I would lose.

I jumped up into the back of my truck pretending to prepare for loading my ATV as I responded in a friendly manner that I was just on a little vacation trying to have a good time. Several times we bantered back and forth. I tried to be friendly but he became more aggressive with each exchange. I tried to divert the deteriorating conversation, but his voice soon reached a high pitch of anger and he stepped forward and slammed his fist into the side of my truck.

Those knuckle prints remained permanently in that truck and were a reminder of the incident as long as I owned it. This action convinced me he intended to put some knuckle prints in me next. This is not good, I thought, as I used my foot to slide my axe out from under the storage box of the truck.

Brutus stepped back a couple of steps giving me the opportunity to quickly pick up my axe. I looked around for help but it was just him and me. I was sure he had every intention of attacking me, so I held up my axe handle and warned him, "Don't touch my truck again or I'll knock your head clear off!"

It wasn't very convincing, even to me, and a cold chill went down my spine, as he didn't say a word but coldly stared into my eyes and motioned with his upturned palms for me to come on! This was a Wild West showdown right out of a Marty Robbins ballad! So I drew first.

I jumped out of the back of my truck, axe-handle high above my head, and came around the end of the truck fast and right at him. Having in the past whacked numerous coyotes with my trowel handle, I had every intention of laying this coyote out cold. However, drunk, schizophrenic or not, Brutus still had enough sense in his thick skull to give ground and back up. He obviously understood what an axe handle could do to one's head.

As he backed away, he started laughing and grinning as if he really didn't mean it and suddenly tried to act friendly. I was having none of it and told him in no uncertain terms to go away and stay away. I then went back to my ATV with the intention of loading it in my truck, but he started to close in on me each time I laid my axe aside. Finally in disgust, I wheeled the ATV around and headed up the road to Jim's house. As I sped off, I noticed Brutus heading for his cabin.

I knocked on Jim's door and reported the incident to him. He asked if I needed help, but I thought the bully would leave me alone now that someone else knew what was going on. I returned to my truck and no one was around. I quickly loaded my ATV, grabbed my gun and secured myself inside the cabin. Now, I thought, maybe that's it. I can now get some rest.

Unfortunately, Brutus had a different idea. He almost immediately started beating on the metal cabinets and yelling obscenities at me through the thin walls. This tantrum went on for some time, but finally he grew quiet and I crawled into bed, wide awake, well-armed and ready for self-defense.

Soon I saw a shadow through the glass of my door and came a quiet knock. It turned out that Jim had decided to call the sheriff, and the deputy slipped quietly in to question me about what had transpired. As the deputy left he turned to ask if I was armed, and when I answered in the affirmative, he admonished me that if anything happened to be sure and "not shoot him!"

The deputy then went outside and after an hour of talking through the door, Brutus allowed the deputy into his cabin and they had a long talk. Satisfied that he had solved the problem, the law departed and all was quiet again.

I started to drift off to sleep when suddenly the cabinet banging and obscenities started in again. It was now 10:00 p.m. and the banging and yelling escalated for the next half hour. I finally reached the end of my patience and decided it was time to get out of there. It seemed obvious this guy was going to blow completely very soon and something very bad would happen.

I had my cell phone inside the cabin and I called 911 hoping to get the deputy to escort me out of the area. Much to my dismay, he was now over an hour away and I was on my own. I grabbed my pistol and big flashlight, opened the door and walked out to my truck. Brutus opened his door a crack and taunted me, but seeing I was well armed he made no attempt to come outside. It was nearly midnight when I checked into a motel in Lakeview for some much needed rest.

Two days later, I checked in with Jim and he had sent Brutus packing for his home turf in another state. Much relieved I moved back into my room and continued my trapline for a few more days. Soon I pulled all my traps and headed for home with Marty Robbins singing his cowboy ballads. The trapping had been great but the catching hadn't been so good. It seems like a lot of my traplines turn out that way. I barely paid the expense of the trip, but the outlaw and the showdown on the high desert made this trip a most memorable experience. I still play Marty Robbins every time I head over the mountains and into cowboy country, where another adventure is sure to be waiting.

Favorite Hunts

Charlie Mock and I were hunting elk near the summit of the Cascade Mountains in late October near where Charlie had hunted the year before. This country was out of my normal hunting area, but since Charlie was familiar with the country we decided to give it a try again this year. We arrived on Friday afternoon and were up early for a good breakfast. Long before daylight we shouldered our day packs and headed west of the Pacific Crest Trail from our camp near Olallie Lake in the Mount Jefferson area.

After a mile or so of travel on the well-established hiking trail we parted company for the day and planned to meet up on this trail sometime in late afternoon. I headed south for a half a mile or so and then continued in a westerly direction. I hunted along slowly, watching for fresh elk tracks, but even old elk sign was almost non-existent and fresh tracks were not to be found.

What I did see was bear sign. Evidence of bears seemed to be everywhere. Every small wet spot or pothole lake had bear tracks of different sizes. A small brown mushroom was blooming on the old growth forest floor and piles of bear scats that looked very much like cow pies were everywhere. In all my years of hunting I had never seen so much bear sign in a small area, and it looked as if bears had come for miles to feed on this rich food source.

I walked for several miles trying to cover lots of ground and maybe stumble onto some elk tracks, but it seemed to me a desolate area for elk. Bear sign continued to be everywhere. One area in particular was downright spooky from all the bear tracks and sign. This area was a huge boulder patch where many of the rocks were as big

185

as automobiles lying quite close together with trails between them. I worked my way through this boulder patch to some open old growth timber and sat down with my back against a tree. A short night's sleep and a long morning of hiking on rough ground had me ready for a good rest, and this park-like setting looked like a good place to take up a stand. Even though I had seen literally piles of bear sign, I was still focused on getting a bull elk and was somewhat discouraged at the lack of any fresh elk tracks.

In the warm afternoon sun the woods had that dead calm silence that often comes in early afternoon when most critters take a midday siesta. It didn't take long for my eyelids to grow heavy and very soon I drifted off into a sound sleep.

CRACK! I couldn't really tell how long I had been asleep but it must have been quite a while. I knew what the noise was before I opened my eyes. I had heard it before and the sound of a bear ripping apart a log is a very distinctive sound. My friend Ralph Flowers had clued me in to the importance of hunting bears by sound in the Coast Range logged-off areas and it is a good tip. I couldn't see a bear when I opened my eyes but it wasn't long before he ambled into view. He was headed directly toward me at about one hundred yards so I just sat quietly and let him come.

I hear a lot about four-hundred-pound bears in my line of work. In fact, almost every truck driver I have ever heard who'd seen a bear run across the road in front of his truck would radio in to anyone who was in CB radio range that he had just seen a four-hundred-pound bear! Many hunters are the same and it seems giant bears are the usual bears that get sighted.

For my part, I have only seen two four-hundred-pound bears (both of which were weighed) in thirty years of bear damage control work and an additional twenty years of hunting. There certainly are Oregon bears that reach four hundred pounds or more. I have seen pictures and have heard first-hand accounts of much bigger bears. Also, most of the bears I have personally viewed were late spring bears that were not at the top of their seasonal weight swing. Nevertheless, four-hundred-plus-pound bears are few and far between in western Oregon.

The bear coming at me was a big brute. He had no idea that I was waiting for him as he slowly worked his way from one rotten log to another and flipped them over or tore them apart looking for grubs. I ever so slowly moved my gun from across my knees into a shooting position.

At about eighty yards he turned broadside and I quickly put the bead behind his front shoulder and squeezed off a shot. The big bruin exploded into a racehorse-like run almost directly at me. I quickly emptied the three other cartridges in my Remington model 742, 30/06 and, in my usual fast shooting pattern, missed all three shots. However, it didn't make any difference, and at the end of a one-hundred-yard sprint the big old boy collapsed into a heap. The first shot was right on target and had taken his heart out.

So much for well-thought-out hunting strategies by the professional bear trapper. I had just taken my biggest ever black bear but the skill involved was somewhat suspect. I did prove that sitting still for an extended period of time in really good bear country is a good way to kill a trophy bear. My best plan of action for killing big game has always been to spend a lot of time in the woods. Nothing takes the place of lots of hunting time to bring on some good luck.

Even though I wasn't really after a bear, this was a good way to start elk season, and Charlie and I had a great piece of meat for winter. It took Charlie and me two days to pack that big bear four miles out to the trailhead, and everything except the entrails was eventually weighed. The final tally of parts added up to 396 pounds of edible meat, head and hide. The weather was somewhat warm, so I decided to take the bear home on Monday to get it into a cooler. Charlie and I rarely split up on our hunts, but in this case I decided to go south about a hundred miles to hunt in a more familiar area, and

Bob Gilman in 1998 with a four-hundred-pound bear taken in the Mount Jefferson Wilderness Area.

Charlie elected to stick it out in the Mount Jefferson area.

It was 11:00 p.m. Monday evening before I got the bear taken care of and stored in a freezer for safe keeping. I would thaw it out later when I had more time to do the butchering. By 11:30 p.m. I had gathered a few more supplies and hit the sack for a few hours of sleep before heading toward Diamond Peak some 150 miles south from home. By 2:00 a.m. the next morning, I had coffee in hand and hit the road. I planned to be hunting up into the Mount Yoran basin on the west side of the Cascade Mountains near Diamond Peak by daylight, so I had no time to waste.

Some three hours later I arrived at the Notch Lake trailhead and parked my truck. It was still dark but two other trucks sat empty in the parking lot. The hunters had already departed up the main trail toward Vivian Lake and Mount Yoran. If you're new to hunting, you will soon find out that most elk hunters are not lazy! In our part of the Pacific Northwest there is no tougher breed of hunters. As a rule they work harder and go farther into rough country in pursuit of their quarry than any other group. The reason, of course, is the prize at the end of the hunt. There just isn't any more magnificent animal or more satisfying endeavor than a successful elk hunt.

I quickly grabbed my day pack with survival gear, extra ammo and a few snacks and headed over the hill into the Swift Creek basin that drains the base of Mount Yoran. In the rush to depart I forgot my little flashlight that usually resides in a side pocket of my pack. I hunted slowly up the basin and part of the time followed the blaze marks of my winter marten trapline. I had spent a lot of time in this basin and knew it was good elk country, but on this day it seemed as devoid of elk sign as the Mount Jefferson area had been on the previous two days.

As the day wore on I worked my way higher and higher until I reached the six-thousand-foot elevation about midday and decided it was time to start back down the mountain. I hadn't bothered to eat

189

breakfast at the early hour I departed home, and the little snacks in my day pack hadn't amounted to much sustenance during the day, although I had had plenty of water from the high mountain springs.

By late afternoon I was really starting to feel the exertion from packing out the bear, a long day and short night, lack of food and then an all-day hike today. More and more I was thinking about getting back to my truck and cooking up a good bite of grub for supper. I was really regretting how far I had come as I trudged out of the basin and back toward the trailhead still some two miles off. At this point I was thinking that maybe I had made a big mistake in not going back up to Mount Jefferson and hunting with Charlie. My head was now down and I didn't have much desire for hunting. I just tried to put one foot in front of the other with the only thought being to get back to the trailhead and my truck, where good food and a warm sleeping bag awaited me.

Suddenly, I stumbled into a brand new pack trail that had been built the previous summer. I didn't know where it was coming from but it was heading northeast and was sure to tie in with the Notch Lake/Vivian Lake trail and would give me an easy route back to the trailhead. This was a very acceptable change of plans from the cross country, brushy, uneven ground that I would need to traverse back to my truck in a straight line. Without breaking stride I started plodding up the trail with only one thing on my mind, and that was to get back to the truck.

I noticed on the new dusty trail a solid set of human prints and it looked like at least a dozen other hunters had hiked the trail today. I continued with much effort to put one foot in front of the other on the slightly uphill trail. A very slight breeze hit me in the face as the trail turned to the north. With my eyes fixed on the dusty trail and without the least particle of energy left in my body, I unexpectedly noticed that the human tracks had turned into elk tracks! These tracks were absolutely fresh, perfect imprints. A quick scan of the tracks revealed a calf, three or four cows and what looked to be a nice-sized bull.

It was simply amazing how quickly I went from completely worn out and bedraggled to feeling full of energy with all senses functioning at full capacity. Hearing, smell and eyesight were all on full alert as I quietly padded up the dead-silent, powder-dusty trail. The shadows were getting long and I knew there wasn't a lot of time to catch these elk.

Knowing that an elk can walk nearly as fast as a man can run, I set off at a fast pace. I hadn't gone 200 yards when I spotted the butt end of an elk calf walking up the trail in front of me. I could hear the other elk as they fanned out ahead of the calf, and by the noise they were making it was evident that they were feeding, didn't know I was around, and were in no hurry.

The calf was a typical kid, lollygagging behind and taking the easy route right up the center of the pack trail. I slowly started gaining on the calf but couldn't see any of the others in the herd. I kept gaining on the calf but the other elk remained just out of my sight and the little fellow kept stopping and fooling around. Each time the calf stopped I would also stop and stand perfectly still hoping that he didn't turn around and look behind him. He didn't seem to have a care in the world and never did look back like a mature elk would have surely done.

I crept up to within about eight feet of the calf and began to think how funny it would be to run up and poke him in the butt with my rifle. I still had not seen any of the other elk. The trail entered into a small thicket of ten-foot-high fir trees and I could only see ahead for a few feet up the trail. Without warning, the little calf took a couple of big jumps as if startled, but I soon discovered he was just hopping around and playing. Nevertheless, when the calf jumped, I thought the jig was up.

I charged up the trail and around a little corner nearly bumping into the back end of the calf. When the calf looked back, big wide eyes were all I could see as he truly flushed this time. It was too late to do anything else, so I just kept running up the trail and, to my surprise, I ran right into the small band of elk no more than forty feet away.

The entire band was caught flatfooted and on this occasion the quarry was more surprised than I was. The five-point bull went left and all the cows went to the right side of the trail, quickly crashing out of sight in the dense trees. The bull now realized that he had been deserted and hooked back to the right, crossing the trail forty-five yards ahead and right in front of me. That was his big mistake. Two quick shots from my 06 and the bull was hit hard. He made a twenty-yard half-moon circle, and one more shot dropped him right in the middle of the pack trail.

The horns on this elk were what big-time elk hunters call a rag horn, but what I call a great trophy. Like most hunters, I get excited over a nice rack of antlers, but as a confirmed life-long meat hunter I prefer prime meat over old horns any day.

The light was fading very fast as I wrestled with getting the big critter field dressed. This is a pretty big job for one person alone, especially when it's getting dark and you are in a big rush. There was no chance of quartering this animal before dark, so as quickly as possible I skinned out the hams and one side of the elk as far down as I could and struggled to get a big limb under the back bone to lift him off the ground just a little. I have never had an elk spoil overnight but have heard enough stories to know it happens pretty easily. By the time I got the elk in good shape, it was very dark and I soon found out that my pack contained no flashlight.

With no light and still a mile from the trailhead I decided to get out to my truck and fill the tag out when I got back to where I could see. I started out the trail and it was about as dark a night as I ever tried to navigate. I went stumbling along very slowly, feeling for the soft center of the trail or the rougher ground at the edge. It was a very long mile, and I was very happy to break out of the deep timber into the open meadow of the trailhead parking lot.

All the other trucks had gone as I slowly climbed into my truck. It had been a very long day. I headed down the road a couple of miles to where a little creek crossed the road and I pulled off the side of the road to make camp.

As quickly as possible I drug out my cooking gear and fixed a big frying pan full of ham, eggs, hash browns and some coffee. I then rolled my sleeping bag out on the ground and climbed in for some badly needed rest. As soon as I lay down I started thinking about my untagged bull elk lying in the middle of the pack trail and the hunters who were sure to arrive early in the morning.

A big full yellow moon was starting to rise as I tried to figure out how I would wake myself up in time to beat those other hunters to my elk. I didn't have a watch with me, but as it turned out I really didn't need one since I lay without sleeping most of the night worrying about waking up in time. I did get a few cat naps but would soon wake up to look at the position of the moon and estimate what time it was. When I finally determined it was a couple of hours till daylight, I got up, ate a quick breakfast, had some strong coffee and departed for the trailhead.

I congratulated myself on getting to the trailhead early enough to beat the stampede of hunters who might like to slap their tag on my elk. This is not unheard of and I was not about to take any chances. I eased back in my truck seat to wait until nearly daylight before hitting the trail to get up to my elk. Unfortunately, the radio now told me that it was only 2:00 a.m., and I had a very long wait.

I pulled my hat down, put a warm coat around me and snuggled down into my seat. The next thing I knew, it was daylight and two rigs had pulled up in the parking lot. They wasted no time when they saw me parked there and all bailed out and immediately hurried off up the trail.

I quickly grabbed my pack board, ropes and butchering equipment and started up the trail at a fast pace. Within a few minutes I saw the guys ahead of me but they saw me and quickened their pace in an attempt to stay ahead of me. Finally, I had to run right up to them and explain that I had an elk laying in the trail up ahead. This didn't make these guys very happy, and I suppose they had been on to this herd the day before.

They left the trail, and I went up and took care of cutting up the elk into manageable pieces to pack out on my back. I made several trips out to the trailhead in the next two days and was a happy hunter with an easy trophy bear and an even easier bull elk for winter meat. Those two big game animals came about as easy as any I ever bagged, but at the time it seemed like an awful lot of work to get an easy elk and an easy bear.

My all-time favorite elk hunt came just one year after my most disastrous elk hunt. Since I prefer to remember the good times, I will tell my most memorable tracking story first.

I was getting around pretty good by elk season, but still just a little gimpy from the previous year's disastrous hunt. That season I had ended up without an elk to eat and on top of that I nearly missed the entire trapping season from injuries received on the hunt. I did finally manage to get one hip boot on and a plastic garbage sack around my cast on the other leg and, with crutches and a little help from Rick Farthing, I was able to set a couple of beaver traps. After catching a couple of beaver I was satisfied and had kept my thirty-plus years of consecutive trapping seasons at least partially intact and pulled my traps.

Charlie and I had hunted together that season, and after the trauma we decided to hunt with a big family group the following year. We also picked some much gentler ground in a more accessible area. The hunt this time was in the Tea Table Mountain country, not too far from Jackie's Thicket and the north end of the great Klamath Marsh. The hunting party included Charlie Mock, my brother-in-law, Steve Erb, my uncle, Jerol Ware, and my mom and dad, Don and Barbara Gilman, along with long-time friend, Paul Carlisle. This was just one of those great family-and-friends hunts with good food, campfires and good story telling. Never mind that I would put a little scare into the camp by not showing up as planned. They all seemed to be a little worried about my health after the previous season.

Paul had been in the area before the elk season started and had spotted a couple of nice bulls. On opening day we made a fool-proof plan and surrounded the large clear-cuts these bulls had been hanging out in. We spotted the bulls at daylight. Brother-in-law Steve happily emptied his rifle at one of these bulls but unhappily watched it get away unscathed. After that, like so many other times when elk make like Houdini, these bulls seemed to just melt away and disappear.

Later that day, Paul took up a stand in a patch of timber for a couple of hours but finally gave up. He hadn't gone more than seventy-five yards when a good bull with several broken antler tines stepped into the trail directly in front of him. Paul was using a new rifle and was unable to find the hidden safety button in the stress of the moment. Like most other bull elk this one didn't spend a lot of time staring at Paul and the jig was up. After the first day, all the elk went into hiding and, though we tromped lots of miles, we couldn't find a bull of any size.

On the third morning of the hunt, I left camp early and drove to a low ridge about two miles away with the intention of hunting my way back to camp by about noon. I hunted slowly back through some good-sized patches of timber finding little fresh elk sign. The weather had been dry so far but a welcome light rain started falling about 8:00 a.m. I had hunted down off the ridges and was in the last big stand of timber before breaking out into a large flat that was about half a mile from our camp.

As I slowly worked my way through the dense timber and brush, I heard the unmistakable sound of an elk pounding right toward me. I immediately got that big game adrenalin rush and jumped up on a large uproot. The brush was very thick in the immediate area and I could only see about twenty feet ahead. It sounded like the elk was going to run right over me and I prepared to shoot in case it turned out to be a legal bull.

As often happens, the elk must have gotten wind of me because just outside my field of vision the elk turned sharply and avoided my position completely. I didn't even get a glimpse of the yellow-tan body as it passed within just a few yards of where I waited. After the elk went by I remained frozen in place just in case there might be more elk coming down the trail.

After about five minutes I heard noises and pretty quick a man came busting through the brush with a wild look on his face. He saw me standing up on the root wad and made the sign with his arms of a set of gigantic antlers. He looked from side to side a couple of times and then darted off in the exact opposite direction that the bull had taken. It didn't take long for me to get off my perch and circle out toward where I had heard the elk. Within five minutes I found the large bull elk prints making twenty-foot bounds and heading up the ridge directly away from camp.

At a walk I followed the tracks for a hundred yards and then settled into a slow jog on the smoking fresh track. I knew from past tracking experience that this bull would put some ground between himself and the hunter he had seen before he would even think about slowing up. The pumice dirt in this area came directly from Mount Mazama, which erupted more than two thousand years ago creating nearby Crater Lake. This pumice is like fine whitish gravel or dirt, and after the morning rain had darkened the surface layer, I could see the dry white pumice for thirty yards in some areas where the elk had kicked it up. The tracking conditions were about as ideal as it gets without snow and I knew I had a good chance at this bull.

The bull kept up the long bounds for 200 yards and then slowed to fast lope for another half mile. This was an area of numerous clear-cuts. The bull headed for each patch of timber between clear-cuts and then stopped inside the tree line before crossing the next clear-cut. After three quarters of a mile the bull slowed to a steady walk and generally headed directly south and into a light breeze. As the bull slowed he became more and more difficult to track, and several times I lost the track and had to go in a large circle until I picked it up again. After two hours of tracking in a southerly direction on rising ground, I left behind the clear cuts and encountered more and more thickets. In each thicket pine needles and forest duff covered the forest floor and made tracking the walking elk exceedingly difficult.

After another half-hour of slow painstaking tracking, the bull fish-hooked hard to the right and took me into a tight thicket of lodge pole pine and ten-foot-tall mixed fir trees. Numerous old elk beds dotted this thicket and I passed several horned up trees. Elk will often do this fishhook pattern when getting ready to bed down for the day. It allows them to check their back trail visually and often they can get the wind drift to tell with that unbelievably sensitive nose whether anything is following them. After winding around in a slow step-by-step hunt the track again fishhooked, this time to the left, and went back to the same southerly pattern it had followed for nearly four miles.

The bull lined out up a ridge and took me by several horned-up trees that I assumed marked a trail he frequently used in his day-to-day travels. I knew I must be getting closer to this elk since he had been moving slowly for some time. As I continued to scrutinize the tracks I realized a second bull had joined the first bull and I was now on the trail of two large bull tracks. I had nearly four-and-a-half miles of tracks behind me and had lost the track completely on several occasions. Each time, I marked the last track location and started circling the area until I once more picked it up. Each time I lost the track, I would think I had lost it for good, but through good luck and persistence I managed to always rediscover the track and get back on course.

When the second bull joined in, the tracking became a little easier, and in another half mile the bulls again fishhooked to the right into a dense thicket. They paralleled their back trail for nearly two hundred yards, off to the west about eighty yards from the original southerly trail. This time the bulls meandered around. I saw evidence of feeding and fresh piles of big black olive elk droppings. I considered this behavior a sure sign the elk were getting ready to bed down.

I hunted very slowly through this thicket and passed several old elk beds and horned-up trees just like the last thicket, but instead of bedding, the bulls returned to the southerly route up a low hogback ridge of pumice. The tracking was again easy and I could see the pair of bull tracks for twenty yards ahead. At five-and-a-half miles, I eased up to the edge of a thicket and stopped in the shadows near a long stretch of open timber. From this vantage point, I was looking at several acres of dense blow-down timber on the far side of the opening some two hundred yards away. It was now after 3:00 p.m. and I had been trailing the first bull since about 9:30 this morning. The bulls had considered bedding down twice, and based on past tracking experience, I was sure they would be bedded in the thicket just ahead.

I backed up slowly and circled nearly half a mile to get on the far side of the blow down and hunt back toward the bulls. It would be futile to try crossing that wide open timber. Even though the wind would be in my favor, those sharp eyes would be trained on their back trail. It took nearly an hour to slowly hunt through the two-hundred-yard thicket of tangled windfall trees one quiet step at a time.

As I approached the far end of the blow down, my anticipation grew with each step. Finally I reached the last thirty yards of cover and realized that the bulls were not in this patch of windfalls. The air went completely out of my sails. Somehow the bulls had given me the slip and I had been beaten again. Even if I could find the tracks it was too late in the day to catch up with these elk again. I was beat!

I put my rifle sling over my shoulder and started out into the long open timber patch that I had observed earlier from the other side of the blow down. As I stomped into the open timber, a small island of brush not more than thirty yards from me and barely ten yards in circumference literally exploded as two beautiful bull elk erupted from this little thicket that I had barely noticed until now.

I have never failed to be amazed at how quickly such large animals can get out of sight and this time was no exception. These bulls caught me completely off guard when I had given up after a long, slow, tense hunt where I had expected them to bolt any second. Those bulls came out of the brush like giant quail and the impact was mentally overwhelming.

Before I could recover, the trailing bull was disappearing into thick timber nearly seventy-five yards below where I was standing. I decided running was my only option so I began sprinting down the slope in the soft pumice soil. I covered over a hundred yards in double-quick time but was well aware of how far a bull elk could run in that same amount of time. This was just an act of sheer desperation on my part. I had little hope of any success, even though I had used this method in the past to kill mule deer bucks that I had jumped and couldn't get a shot off before they were out of sight.

As I burst through a small thicket of head-high fir trees, I was shocked to see one of the bulls standing broadside not forty yards from me. He was looking intently in the direction he was headed, and I suspect he was thinking he had outrun me and was more concerned about something he smelled. At any rate it didn't take him long to decide where the immediate danger was coming from.

This bull didn't jump but crouched down slightly, then acted as if he were shot out of a cannon. This time I was ready and squeezed off two fast shots before the bull hit the brush some twenty feet from where he launched.

It was now only an hour and a half until dark, so I quickly ran to the trail where the bull had departed with no apparent bullet wounds. I searched quickly down the trail and to my surprise found one small drop of blood dead center in the trail. I followed the tracks with a growing sense of frustration and hopelessness. In the past I had trailed numerous elk still going for miles with what seemed like gallons of blood pouring out of them. I knew there was little hope of tracking this bull down tonight but, nevertheless, I stayed on the track for another fifty yards and then I spotted him.

He was standing broadside at about 125 yards in open timber. Again, I wasted little time. This time one shot behind the shoulder with a 165 grain Grand Slam bullet dropped him in his tracks. Some seven hours after I had started tracking this bull I finally had him on the ground. I could hardly believe my good fortune after losing his track so many times, having made so many mistakes and believing that all was lost.

As I lifted the elk's back leg and tied it to a tree to help with the gutting process, I noticed a strip of red across the bull's stomach just a half inch in front of his "important business equipment." I had drawn blood when I jumped the bull the last time, and it was obviously in a place that distracted the bull just enough for me to get one last shot. Persistence, determination and a lot of luck had paid big dividends on this day.

I gutted the animal, skinned out the hams toward the backbone and also skinned one complete side to the backbone. This would allow the big critter to cool down overnight, and there would be no chance for the prime meat to sour as it could under the unbelievable insulating ability of the thick elk hide. I could finish skinning and quarter the animal tomorrow when I had lots of daylight and time. The temperature had been dropping all afternoon and before I finished opening up the elk it started snowing. Very quickly everything began to turn white.

The curtain of darkness was now quickly falling. I heard signal shots several miles away and was sure my hunting party was already looking for me. I was several miles from camp and I knew that I would never find this animal again if I left it now. I quickly decided to spend the night here if necessary. It was most important right now to get a fire started and I rushed around looking for some dry wood under the layer of wet snow that now blanketed the ground. With help from some shavings of black pitch from my pack I soon nursed a small flame into a blazing campfire and gathered a good pile of wood. I pulled out a space blanket and scooped a dry place to set from a low dirt bank.

Now that it was completely dark I fired off three quick shots to make contact with my party. It was soon obvious that someone was listening. I could barely hear answering shots from a long distance north of my position. I fired two more shots to let them know I had heard them and then settled down next to my fire. I pulled the space blanket around me like a tent, pulled a piece of jerky and bottle of water from my pack and leaned back to enjoy the warmth of the cheery fire.

What a great day it had been; many exciting hours of dry ground tracking of one of North America's most elusive and intelligent big game animals. For me, it is difficult to imagine a more challenging hunt than matching wits one-on-one with a mature bull elk on his turf and terms. This had been the most satisfying day of my hunting life and, quite honestly, I was in no hurry to be found. I leaned back

Pictured (from left) on a favorite hunt: Charlie Mock, Steve Erb, Bob Gilman, Don Gilman, Barbara Gilman and Jerol Ware.

and watched the large white snowflakes float to the ground in the glow of the fire. What a difference from the previous season. On the third day of my hunt, a dozen miles of tracking in snow had ended with two six-point bulls getting up out of their beds forty feet from me, and then disaster struck!

Yes, this was much different. I basked in the warmth of the fire and relived every step of the day's hunt. A few hours later my worried mom and dad showed up after driving many miles of dead-end roads, their concerns for a potentially lost or hurt hunter finally relieved. Tomorrow would be the day to get the meat back to camp and take a few pictures. The pictures, memories and stories would last a lifetime.

Charlie in Survival Mode

In early November of 1973, twenty-three-year-old Charlie Mock was right where he wanted to be. Deep in a roadless area of the Mt. Hood National Forest of the Oregon Cascades, snug and warm inside his down bag and underneath a light tarp rigged as a makeshift tent. Tomorrow would bring a full day of hunting for deer or bear, whichever might make its appearance. For now he would get a good night's rest.

The strenuous exercise of the six-mile hike and thousand-foot climb from the Wahtum Lake trailhead to the Mud Lake area had drained some of his youthful energy. After a quick pre-packaged meal, just before dark, Charlie had turned in. A few sparse snowflakes were drifting out of a twenty-five-degree, dark, cloudy sky as Charlie slipped into a comfortable slumber. During the night he had momentarily awakened and noticed a slight weight on his chest, but sleep quickly overcame him and he slept soundly throughout the night.

Charlie had been preparing for this lifestyle for many years. His boyhood days had been spent in the mountains of western Pennsylvania, where he had been obsessed with hunting, fishing, trapping and dreaming of a wilderness lifestyle in some remote area with few people. Like many rural boys of his age he had read every far north and survival-style book he could get his hands on. Two favorites had been *Three Against the Wilderness* and *The Art of Survival*. Every possible minute was spent in the outdoors practicing his neophyte skills.

After graduating from Penn State University in 1969 with a

degree in forestry, Charlie acquired a job with the U.S. Forest Service and headed for the tall and uncut of the Oregon Country, excited about starting his new career out west. After a year with the USFS in the Columbia Gorge District, Charlie was drafted and spent the next two years serving his country in the U.S. Army.

After his discharge in 1971, Charlie returned to his former job with the Forest Service, and in the fall of 1973 he was back in the high mountains of the Oregon backcountry, ready to put to the test the outdoor skills he had been studying and learning about throughout the years. As it turned out, the testing would be a little more than Charlie had bargained for. The knowledge gleaned from those well-worn survival manuals would come in handy in the next few days. At this point in Charlie's life, almost every activity revolved around hunting, fishing, trapping and a subsistence style of living.

It was just breaking day as Charlie roused from a sound sleep and found his little tarp was sagging down on his chest and nearly touching his face. Something was definitely amiss, and a quick look out the end of the tarp enclosure revealed an unsettling sight. Charlie nearly panicked at what he saw. The cool and comfortable late fall of yesterday was gone, and the cold, stark winter had arrived with a vengeance. Twenty inches of fresh wet snow covered the entire landscape and it was snowing hard.

Charlie knew instantly that he was in serious trouble. This storm turned out to be the most severe early season storm to hit the mountains of the Pacific Northwest in many years. Several people were stranded and would be rescued. One young woman, baby in arms, would die from the deadly effects of this unexpected weather system.

Before crawling out of his warm nest, Charlie shuffled through several scenarios of steps he might take to escape the clutches of this powerful storm in this remote area. He was in the Herman Creek basin, six miles from his truck and twenty miles from the nearest help.

204

There was a thousand-foot climb over the ridge and then a thousand-foot decent just to get to his truck. He didn't know what to expect when he got to his truck, but the possibilities didn't look good.

Charlie quickly pulled on his boots and stuffed the meager camping gear into his backpack. In the space of a few hours Charlie had gone from an enjoyable late fall hunting trip into full survival mode. After taking stock of his food supply, Charlie decided to conserve what little he had and departed without any breakfast. The chances were very slim that he would be driving out of this high country, even if he did make it back to his truck.

A steady snowfall continued to float down in huge white flakes as Charlie started the slow strenuous climb out of the basin toward the divide. He was soon in cold, wet, waist-deep snow. It was nearly mid-day by the time he reached the ridge summit and wearily slogged downhill on the last three-mile leg to the trailhead.

Hunger was already gnawing at his empty stomach. The late afternoon light was waning as Charlie staggered through the deep snow and out into the clear-cut where the trailhead was located. He was soaking wet and completely exhausted, and what he saw was not encouraging. His little two-wheel-drive truck was buried almost to the hood.

His worst fears were confirmed and Charlie knew immediately that this truck was going nowhere. The snow had kept piling up and was too deep, even for a young athletic woodsman to navigate without assistance. As he had feared, he would need to develop a different plan to escape the high country.

Charlie removed his pack, cleaned the snow from around the tailpipe, started up the little truck and fell into the driver seat. It didn't take long to get some heat going and it felt mighty good just to get into a warm dry spot to think through the situation he was in. He had, at first, assumed that someone would be coming to rescue him. His friends in the Forest Service knew the trailhead where he had parked, but then he remembered telling them not to worry if he stayed in the mountains a few extra days.

Charlie turned on the truck radio and was barely able to get the static-filled Hood River station. The big weather event had made for a major news story, and the radio announcer told of surprised hunters and travelers around the Pacific Northwest who were stranded or missing because of this massive early-season snowstorm.

Charlie's name did not come up in the list of known stranded or missing people, and this self-sufficient hunter had no thought of waiting this out with the hopes that someone would eventually come to his rescue. He would have to do this himself. The survival wheels were turning and Charlie soon started to develop a plan to extract him from this dangerous situation.

Sunday had been a long exhausting day, but it still remained for Charlie to pitch a quick make-do camp for the night. Two hundred yards from the pickup and in the heavy timber Charlie found a place to string up his tarp and get in out of the snow for the night. He then built a roaring hot fire to get some warmth back in his body and dry his wet clothing. He would have a dry and warm place to sleep tonight, but he was by this time getting mighty hungry.

On Monday morning, Charlie's first order of business was to plan how to stretch the scant food supply. The list included: one helping of dehydrated scrambled eggs, a small quantity of Bisquick, a pre-packaged freeze-dried meal, a small chunk of cheese, dried apples, sugar and tea bags. During Sunday's struggle out of the Herman Creek basin, Charlie had devoured one little three-ounce can of dried fruit. Monday morning's breakfast would be the dehydrated scrambled eggs. With the future uncertain, the slight food supply would be hoarded and a growling stomach would be his companion. He planned to keep his small stash of food for an energy boost before and during the long hike out to civilization. With the calories that Charlie had been burning, he could easily have eaten the entire hoard in one small meal.

A sheltered location was soon found and a good lean-to shelter was constructed with his seven-by-nine-foot tarp and then covered with bows for added protection. Charlie worked steadily and by mid-day had completed a comfortable camp that included a reflector fireplace and deep bow bed on which to place his sleeping pad and down bag. This protection from the elements assured Charlie of being warm and comfortable for the time he would need to stay at this location. After the camp was complete, Charlie took his axe and cut plenty of standing dry poles for a good supply of firewood. The effort of building and supplying the camp took the entire day on Monday.

The camp completed, Charlie's thoughts turned to getting something to eat, a thought that had never left his mind for the last twenty-four hours. With a good knowledge of local plant life, Charlie was able to locate an elderberry bush mostly buried in snow. From this bush he obtained the last remaining clusters of ripe berries preserved under the deep snow. With his last dose of sugar, a sort of elderberry gruel was boiled over the campfire and, although not the best of cuisine, it was edible and did to some degree fill up the hollow spots. This was Charlie's only meal on Monday and a small amount was left over for Tuesday's entire food intake.

Monday evening, Charlie started to institute the plan he had been developing. It was a simple plan: build some snowshoes and walk out of the mountains. Charlie had only been on snowshoes one time in his life but he did know how they worked and what they looked like. With the confidence of youth, the mental notes from several survival manuals and compelled by necessity, Charlie waded out into the deep snow and found four small but tough fir trees to use for frames.

Back in camp with his axe, he proceeded to size and square up the frame pieces, cut slats for spreader bars and then laboriously notch each cross piece and the main frames. This work lasted long

207

into the evening around the campfire. Staying busy with his plan of action, kept Charlie from worrying about what tomorrow would bring. It didn't help with the hunger.

On Tuesday morning, Charlie went right back to work on the snowshoes. The ends of two of the frames were lashed together and the spreader bars were sprung into their notched positions. Charlie's old army pack had been dismantled to use buckles, straps and cordage for lashing all the individual pieces securely in place. The two pairs of squared stems, when completed, were heavy and a little rough, but when lashed together the stout green frames looked about halfway professional. Charlie was encouraged with the quality of the frames. Now if he could only figure out some way of lacing them.

Webbing was a significant problem and Charlie thought long and hard about what he could use. Finally after much consideration he reluctantly removed the rubber floor covering from his brand new truck and laboriously cut it into strips to use for webbing.

Charlie worked late Tuesday evening in the frustrating first attempt to lace webbing into the snowshoe frames. It proved to be a difficult job with the limited supplies that were available to him. The rubber floor mat was a poor substitute for rawhide and, when cut into strips, was quite fragile.

After many attempts, failures and re-calculations, Charlie finally managed to get part of one snowshoe laced up before turning in for the night. The rubber floor mat lacing looked pretty good and might just work. Charlie resolved to finish his snowshoes tomorrow and make the attempt to get out of the high country.

Sleep did not come easily. The small amount of elderberry gruel had worn off many hours before and hunger would be foremost in his mind throughout this night.

Early Wednesday morning, Charlie continued working feverishly to finish lacing the newly manufactured "Cascade Model" snowshoes. After the lacing was finished he lashed them securely to his boots for a short test hike. The snowshoes were a little awkward and the green frames were heavy, but they actually worked quite well! Charlie, with no previous experience at survival in deep snow, had taken the time and used his ingenuity to make a very serviceable pair of emergency snowshoes.

His years of studying and practicing survival skills as a boy in Pennsylvania turned out to be time well spent. Only two questions remained to be answered. Would a pair of snowshoes manufactured under survival conditions, hastily made with makeshift supplies, hold up to a long forced march through the notorious heavy wet snow of the Oregon Cascades? Would Charlie hold up?

Charlie cooked and quickly devoured his freeze-dried food, his first meal of substance since Saturday evening. He hoped this would give him the necessary energy to make the difficult thirteen-mile trek down the remote mountain to safety. By noon he had his axe, space blanket and tarp packed. All other gear was left behind. He would take minimal equipment and go for broke on this hike.

Anyone who has ever traveled for a dozen or more miles on professionally manufactured snowshoes, in good snow conditions, will tell you it is a very good workout. That same hike on new, soft, wet snow, where you sink half way to your knees and pick up several pounds of wet snow with each step, is a grueling test of strength and endurance. If you add to that scenario a pair of heavy, awkward, quickly improvised snowshoes, someone completely unaccustomed to traveling in this manner and with a small intake of calories in the past three days, you have a difficult struggle ahead of you.

Charlie's thirteen-mile trudge to safety took a full thirteen hours. It was a long, hungry and exhausting hike and took every ounce of strength and determination he possessed. The makeshift snowshoes had proven their worth and required only minimal adjustments during the hike.

Later that morning, long-time mountain rescue and survival expert L. C. Baldwin, on his way to find Charlie, found the shoes stuck in the snow where Charlie had abandoned them upon reaching easier going. Baldwin later described them as the best emergency models he had ever seen.

Charlie's survival story was printed in the *Sunday Oregonian* on December 13, 1973, and was later reprinted in *Field & Stream* magazine as "One Survived While Others Died." *Argosy* magazine and *Readers Digest* later ran versions of the story. Several years later, the article was again published in a special addition of a *Field & Stream Classics* magazine.

Charlie had made his self-rescue look almost easy. Experienced outdoors men and women realized, however, that this was an exceptional survival story. Charlie wasn't a highly-trained expert, but rather a self-trained, competent woodsman who stayed calm, used common sense, made smart decisions and didn't panic in the face of a difficult situation.

Charlie still has that old set of snowshoes stored in the rafters of his garage, an occasional reminder of just one of the many memories from a lifetime of outdoor experiences. Many more years of hunting and trapping have given Charlie ample opportunity to continue practicing his outdoor and survival skills since his deep snow adventure in 1973.

I first met Charlie in 1977, and we have been good friends, hunting, fishing, trapping and working partners, ever since that time. We have experienced many fine adventures together. But it wasn't until 1993, when things went all wrong on a hunting trip, that I found out how important it is to have a calm, reliable and skilled outdoorsman for a partner. When I needed help, Charlie Mock was there, in full rescue mode.

Charlie's "Cascade Model" snowshoes

Tribute to a Partner

The tracks turned abruptly uphill toward a dense thicket of mahogany brush, and I knew that after seven hours of steady tracking, my quarry was very close. Slowly I eased up the hill with the soft snow muffling each step and the cold, gusty wind in my face. Silently and at thirty yards, two six-point bulls lurched up from their beds and stood broadside with a surprised look, as if trying to comprehend where I had come from. My Remington semi-automatic 30-06 held a perfect sight picture as I watched them turn and melt into the dense mahogany thicket. At that moment, I felt the entire hunting trip was worthwhile. Even though I had only an antlerless elk tag in my pocket, there isn't a greater hunting thrill to me than beating a bull elk at its own game. Two mature bulls made the thrill even better. Game over. I had won.

I hadn't checked in with Charlie for over an hour, but I knew he would feel as I did. It was about time to give up for the day and try again tomorrow. My hips ached, my knees were weak, and several miles of rough, unknown country separated us from our vehicles. I was sure Charlie was even more exhausted than I, but as I was about to find out, the body can be exhausted, but some men are mentally prepared to continue well past that point. Lucky for me, my friend and long-time hunting partner Charlie Mock, is just such a man.

After the bulls disappeared, I turned toward a hogback ridge a few yards away to get a better view of the area. As I turned, my right foot slipped on an ice-covered rock. I fell over backwards and my leg crumpled beneath me with a sickening pop. The pain took away my breath as I lay on the frozen ground for several minutes, unable to move. As my head began to clear, I knew I was in a bad situation. My next thought was of Charlie, and I hoped he was still somewhere close by. Rolling out of my day pack, I fished out the small CB. "Charlie, Charlie, Charlie," I called over the radio. My stomach turned when I got no response.

As I had started this hunt it was late November of 1993, and two inches of fresh snow blanketed the ground on top of Arrowwood Point forty miles southeast of Prineville. I had hunted alone on Saturday and Sunday and Charlie had arrived in camp late Sunday night. Monday morning the high desert temperature was in the low twenties, and the forecast was for a severe Arctic storm to hit sometime later in the day, with increasing snowfall and temperatures dipping below zero.

An hour before daylight Charlie and I had struck fresh tracks going into a logged-off area. I grabbed my flashlight and began tracking the elk while Charlie stayed on the road. Forty minutes later the tracks had led me on a winding path that eventually came back to the road where I found Charlie patiently waiting for me. Full daylight had come as we shouldered our well-worn day packs and set out in earnest to fill our cow tags.

The country was new to us, but it was with complete confidence built on many years of working, hunting and trapping together that we set out at a fast pace, determined to catch our prey. I adjusted my pack several times in the first mile and thought the extra weight of the handheld CB radio, the small hatchet, and other equipment, twelve pounds in all, seemed excessive. Little did I know how important many of these items were going to be before this day would end. This would be the first time I had ever carried a hand held radio while hunting.

Charlie started trailing while I paralleled his course about three hundred yards uphill and slightly ahead, hoping to get a shot if the elk turned my way. We jumped the small band in the first hour but they were just out of sight over a juniper ridge. When I hit the fresh bounding tracks, I began to pursue at a dog trot, and caught them two miles farther as they stopped to catch their wind in a mahogany thicket. A fat cow showed herself broadside at seventy-five yards. I couldn't believe it when the cow kept going, but the dense brush had evidently deflected my shot. The snow showed no sign of a hit.

The elk then turned into the wind and lined out across the high desert. I checked with Charlie on the CB as I caught my breath and found he was following my tracks close behind. The insulated bib overalls and jacket, which had felt so good earlier that morning, were now providing way too much warmth. I stowed the jacket in my pack and unzipped the legs of the bibs to allow for ventilation and again took pursuit.

I had known Charlie for over fifteen years, and for eight of those years we worked side by side for several months of each season, trapping mountain beaver that were causing damage to timber companies in the rugged Coast Range mountains of western Oregon. In that time, we had become close friends with many memorable campfires behind us. When you work with someone under difficult and extreme conditions, you learn their abilities very well and I knew that Charlie's abilities were substantial. Over the years he has almost always outworked, out-walked and outdone me in general. At this particular time, however, I felt I was in better physical condition than he. His commercial bee business required long hours and hard work, but not necessarily the kind that puts you in good shape for hunting. My fall season had been much different. A contract with the Oregon Department of Fish and Wildlife to capture bears for a long-term population study, along with contracts for private companies doing a variety of animal damage control work, required lots of hiking and had kept me in excellent physical condition.

At 11:00 a.m., we crossed a seldom-used dirt road and stopped to eat a candy bar and drink some juice. Five minutes later, with over six miles of sagebrush and rim rock behind us, I took the tracks again as Charlie paralleled two hundred yards to my left. We were beginning to feel the strain of the rough going, but the elk were also starting to tire and had tried to bed three times. Over the next three miles, the elk took us into the most rugged country of the day, consisting of steep treacherous rockslides with dense mahogany brush thickets.

A half mile farther, two elk jumped fifty yards above me and disappeared. I left the tracks I was following and gave chase but realized after a few hundred yards that these were not the same tired elk we had tracked since early morning. I stood still for a moment trying to decide whether to continue on or backtrack to the original bunch, but the hot tracks in front of me were just too tempting. I rationalized that Charlie was close behind and would continue to follow the original bunch, giving us the opportunity to fill both our tags. I followed the tracks for another mile, then they turned abruptly uphill and into the mahogany thicket. It was here I jumped the two bulls.

As I lay on the snow-covered rocks, waves of pain throbbed up my broken leg. Looking down, I realized my right foot was turned out at a strange angle, obviously severely dislocated.

After calling several times on the CB, I reached for my gun, cleaned the snow out of the action and fired three quick shots. Then I tried the CB again and Charlie's familiar voice came over the radio. A few minutes later I was greatly relieved to see him struggle up the steep sidehill to me. The tired and distressed look on his face told the story we both knew. We were in a very serious situation and had no time to lose.

It was 12:15 p.m., snow was starting to fall, and the temperature was dropping fast. Charlie examined my leg and began to cut a splint while I rummaged through my day pack to take my mind off the pain. I gritted my teeth as Charlie bound two sticks tightly to my leg and foot to stabilize it.

He then went to a low-limbed juniper tree a few feet away and scooped up a large pile of dry duff for a bed. He cut a small bunch of juniper bows and placed them on top of this for added insulation. He then placed me on the bed of dry needles that gave at least some protection from the cold ground and cutting wind. I downed several aspirin as he laid an extra coat over my chest and put both our packs within my reach.

Charlie grabbed a roll of bright pink flagging from my pack for marking a trail and set out for help. The first quarter mile of his route was up a steep rockslide and ledge rock mountain covered with snow and ice. Charlie was nearly done in when he reached the top but continued to stumble across the frozen juniper and mahogany mountains for three miles until he fortunately hit the end of the nearest road.

It was 2:00 p.m., and Charlie had now hiked over fifteen miles since daybreak. The road gave him encouragement, and at 3:00 p.m. with another three miles of trail behind him, Charlie stumbled into the camp of four experienced elk hunters.

Left alone and lying on a windswept juniper ridge, I took account of the situation. I was well prepared for the weather conditions. Warm rubber-bottomed insulated packs were on my feet along with thick wool socks. Added to that were thermal underwear, loose-fitting blue jeans, a flannel shirt, warm hat and insulated gloves. Most importantly, I had a pair of Walls insulated bib overalls and a blizzard-proof coat just purchased for this trip. With these layers of clothing I felt almost comfortable, but the shock would still occasionally cause me to shake uncontrollably.

I continued to rummage through my pack and found a space blanket that I had carried for several years. Taking my time, I slowly unraveled the thin blanket of coated plastic and spread it over my legs and chest. The impact of this flimsy blanket was unbelievable. Within minutes I felt as if I were in a warm sleeping bag. I dared not

Charlie makes me comfortable and then heads out several miles for help.
Illustration by Sharon Davis

move, however, for fear of tearing the thin covering.

The wind picked up and visibility dropped to a few yards as snow began to cover me, but it only added more insulation and warmth. I had a mental picture of how I would look to a rescue party. Except for my face, I was completely covered with snow. Without the layers of special clothing and space blanket, hypothermia would have been a major problem. I wasn't hungry but forced down a candy bar, raisins and some juice to help produce heat and waited long hours hoping help would arrive.

Gordon Falgren, his two sons, Ken and Ray, and their hunting partner, Cliff Kiser, had arrived back at camp in early afternoon and decided to wait out a predicted snowstorm instead of taking an afternoon hunt. Then Charlie staggered into their camp. It took only minutes for these able hunters to make a plan and react. Gordon took Charlie the seven miles to our vehicles where Charlie had a cellular telephone. Gordon then drove fifteen miles to a main road to meet an ambulance.

Charlie went on to my truck where we had an ATV, and then he headed back for the end of the road. Meanwhile, Cliff, Ken and Ray loaded Cliff's three horses into the trailer and started back to the end of the road, taking with them a sleeping bag, first-aid kit and other rescue gear.

At 4:00 p.m., I was trying to gather what dry juniper limbs I could reach in order to build a fire. Darkness was only an hour away and I was starting to mentally prepare for a long night.

Then I heard my name called out from far above, and within minutes Ray, Ken and Cliff arrived. Cliff carefully removed Charlie's temporary splint and Ken helped hold the bones in place as an air bag splint was placed around my leg and blown up. Unfortunately, this air splint was full of holes. Cliff, using his early Boy Scout training, securely splinted the leg with new sticks in preparation for the long trip out. Ray, in the meantime, had cut two poles for a litter, and all extra coats and shirts were threaded on them.

By this time, Charlie, using the ATV, had reached the place where the horses were tied, then hiked the four hundred yards down to my location. Darkness fell as they hoisted my stretcher and we started out. I didn't realize until later that it would have been impossible for only three men to pack me up that mountain. Each step up the dark rockslide was a gut wrenching challenge for the four men, and they could manage only a few steps without rest.

Charlie had again shown his value as a friend and partner. He later told me that carrying me up that mountain was one of the hardest things he had ever done.

An hour later, I was lifted over the last rock ledge and onto the plateau where the horses were tied. With a good deal of help, I mounted Cliff's horse, Misty, and we followed a compass line for a longest three-mile horseback ride of my life. A bitter wind blew out of the north and heavy snow reduced visibility to a few yards. I hunched over the saddle horn and tried to hang on.

At 8:00 p.m., we arrived where rescue vehicles waited. There was much concern that I might be suffering from hypothermia, but the quality layered clothing I wore had served its purpose well. I had no lasting effects from the subfreezing weather, even though it would be several months before I regained the complete use of my right leg. Eleven hours after the fall, we arrived at the emergency room and the worst was over.

In the course of the long and painful day, I had the opportunity to check out my survival gear, much of which I had carried for many years. Some items, such as the marking ribbon and CB radio, were of major importance for a quick rescue. Other items, such as the space blanket, added greatly to my comfort and protection from the elements.

Basic survival gear that I always carry included compass, matches, hatchet, a small bundle of pitch wood, candle stub, extra food and a small flashlight. I had not needed these items but they were ready for use had I not been rescued that day. I was very fortunate when Charlie made it safely to the camp of Gordon, Ken and Ray Falgren, and Cliff Kiser. They are just the kind of hunters you like to find when the chips are down.

My friend and hunting partner stood above the rest. Had I been hunting alone in that remote part of the Oregon high desert, my bones could very likely still be there! I highly recommend a good partner as the very best survival gear.

The Bear Trappers

This book would not be complete without mention of the numerous trappers who have worked for me over the last thirty years. I have written about a few incidents with some of these guys but have barely scratched the surface of available stories. Many of these fellow trappers and hunters could easily write books themselves. Most of them are not mentioned by name in the stories but I include some of them here to give recognition. Just because I haven't written a story about a certain trapper does not indicate that they weren't an important part of my life and career. Many of the trappers listed have been lifelong friends. Several of them are "real characters."

The statement "worked for me" is a bit of an exaggeration in some cases. It is true enough that I was the employer and could hire and fire, but seasoned trappers are a very independent lot. A better description of our relationship would be "worked with," and most of the time that was the way I approached their employment.

Several of the older trappers I hired had thirty to forty years of trapping experience before joining my crew. All I did was provide equipment, give them the criteria for taking bear or other animals, show them their area and get out of the way.

Some of the trappers worked for only one season, but others, like Andy Johnson, Dave Vann, Ray Jordan, Joe Colver, Terry Sawyer, Denny Schutz and Dean Bartz came back for several years of seasonal work. A few, like Paul Carlisle, Sam Gilman and Matt Peterson, worked as full-time trappers for many years. We worked together while I was contracted by Northwest Animal Damage Cooperative and other individual companies. I include here brief sketches of a few of the fellows.

From the beginning, my strategy for hiring employees for animal damage control work was to hire people who were at least as good at trapping as I. I mostly succeeded in this strategy and in many cases they were much better trappers than I. This made my life pretty easy since these guys were already self-motivated experts and needed no prodding to capture bears or other wildlife that were causing property damage. I tried to keep a respectful distance between the employer/employee relationship and personal friendships. I failed in this respect, and count many former employees and foresters I worked with as lifelong friends. Come to think of it, that is not such a failure.

Generally, the following sketches fall in no particular order of importance, except for the first couple of guys. They are special for several reasons. First is my son, Sam, who followed me into the animal control and trapping business. Second is Paul Carlisle. Paul worked for me longer than any other employee except Sam and was nearly full-time for several years. The others follow randomly as they came to mind. I haven't covered every employee I hired, but that doesn't imply they weren't worthy. It could be that they were just very good at what they did and didn't end up in any predicaments or situations that would make a good story.

Sam Gilman

Sam grew up around trapping and as a young boy he went with me to check traps on numerous occasions. Trapping didn't seem to stick with Sam and as he grew up he drifted into other interests. Sam is an avid fly fisherman and was tying and selling hand tied flies when he was fourteen years old. He also enjoyed hunting, but one of his greatest interests has always been to follow football and basketball teams. As Sam grew up and got out on his own it didn't look like he

A few of the "Bear Trappers" (from left): Paul Carlisle, Bob Gilman, Ray Jordan, Sam Gilman, Dave Vann, Matt Peterson and Andy Johnson.

would ever follow in my footsteps.

Sam had lots of different jobs for a few years and they all seemed to go nowhere. As a last resort Sam came to me and asked for a job. I was contracting mountain beaver trapping at the time and gave Sam an opportunity to try out. After a few days Sam had enough of this kind of hard work and decided to try some other line to make a living. Again after a few months Sam came back and asked for a job. This time he knew what he was getting into and went to work for me on a hot September day in 1996.

Mountain beaver trapping is difficult physical work. The logged-off units that we trapped were steep and brushy or if we were lucky they would be burned. Burned units would turn us as black as soot but had much less brush to fight through. The unit that Sam started on was called Palo Mountain on Starker Forests property near Alsea. By the time Sam started trapping I no longer did the actual boomer trapping. Paul Carlisle was working for me and he did most of the boomer trapping. I hired Sam to be his helper but I held out little hope that he would make the grade this time around. Sam and Paul dropped off into the big canyon to spend the day setting boomer traps and I went to do some other business. I came back to the landing at the end of the day and arrived just as Sam was coming up over the edge of the landing. He was sweating profusely and looked as if one more step up that steep mountain would cause him to collapse. I really figured he would quit at the end of that day.

As it turned out, Sam did make the grade. From that day forward, he took to trapping like he was made for it and never looked back. He eventually became one of my best boomer trappers and ended up running a crew and our boomer camp for several seasons. Sam later started trapping bears for me and soon became one of my most dependable and skilled bear trappers.

When I started a new company called Ketch-Um Wildlife Control in 2004, Sam quickly became the key employee and very soon was running all the field operations of this small business. Sam became an expert in all kinds of urban wildlife control and continues working full time in the animal control business today. I am sure that I never encouraged Sam enough or told him often enough that he was doing a great job. Just let me say right here and now how proud I am of my son. His work ethic is superb, he is an expert at his trade, and he is honest and treats his clients with respect. At the time of this writing Sam has worked for me and with me for over eighteen years. Most importantly, he has a great family (a wife and five of my grandchildren) and we have a great relationship. What more could a father ask?

Paul Carlisle

Just like me and lots of other would-be trappers, Paul Carlisle picked up a copy of *Fur-Fish-Game* magazine when he was about twelve or thirteen. Trapping looked very interesting to a country boy in Illinois. Paul's dad didn't trap or know anything about it, but his grandpa had trapped as a kid in Minnesota. Paul wrote a little sketch of his trapline history and I thought it would be good to include it here. Paul's story of growing up and learning about trapping is representative of many others who worked for me over the years.

"I probably caught a total of ten rats in two years in Illinois where I grew up as a young boy. We moved to Oregon when I was fifteen, and I trapped beaver and muskrats around Bend for the two years that we were there. We then moved to the Kinzua area near Fossil where I did a little beaver trapping.

"Later after I was married and moved to Springfield, I met Blaine Miller. At that time I operated an auto repair shop and Blaine brought his pickup in for work. Blaine was a lifelong trapper and well known for his nutria trapping expertise in the Willamette Valley. My association with Blaine rekindled the trapping fire and I started trapping again in 1979 after a twelve-year break. I trapped for beaver and cats (poorly, I might add). I caught a few beaver a year for a number of years until I finally figured out that there were lots of beaver located between the Willamette Valley, where I lived, and the Oregon coast. My first effort on the Siuslaw and Smith rivers netted about fifty beaver and half a dozen otter in a week.

"I have probably caught more than a thousand beaver over the years. During my first year of trapping on Green's Island on the Willamette River I caught nearly four hundred nutria. In my years of bear work I also took quite a few cougars. All of the cougars except one were taken as incidental to bear damage control and released."

Paul Carlisle traveled with Gilman's and Ketch-Um Wildlife

Control for many years. In those years Paul did most of the boomer trapping for GWC, carried out a major river beaver control contract for several years and had the responsibility for bear damage control in two of our most important districts. Paul also captured bears when GWC contracted with the Oregon Department of Fish and Wildlife for a major bear study in the Cascade Mountains. As I recall, Scott Sweringen and Paul captured seventy-two bears in two seasons of work for the ODFW bear study. At times and when needed Paul was Gilman's mechanic, shop organizer and trap repair specialist. When we started a second business, Ketch-Um Wildlife Control, to do urban work, Paul worked for both Gilman's Inc. and Ketch-Um for several years. His hard work, dedication, dependability and skills as a trapper were important reasons for the long-term success of our businesses. It is a fair statement that Paul and I grew up together in the bear and urban damage control business.

Anders (Andy) Johnson

Andy Johnson went to Montana from his home state of Minnesota in 1986 at nineteen years of age, and then moved on to Wyoming in 1989. He started out working for dude ranches and cattle outfits, then graduated to the outfitting industry as a hunting guide. His first dude ranch job was at the Elkhorn Ranch in the Gallatin Canyon, and his first guiding job was for the 320 Ranch, also in the Gallatin Canyon. Andy first worked as a guide in Wyoming for Cabin Creek Outfitters who operated Buffalo Bill's original hunting camp up the North Fork of the Shoshone, Camp Monoco. Andy always enjoyed seeing new country and, therefore, worked for several different outfits in the Cody area. One of his favorite regions was the Thorofare where he spent a good deal of time guiding hunters.

Andy also helped outfitter Rick Felts of the Grizzly Ranch with summer pack trips through the back country of Yellowstone. I had the pleasure of accompanying Rick and Andy along with several of

Andy's family members on one of these enjoyable summer pack trips.

By the time I met Andy in 1996, he was a seasoned guide with experience that included stints in Wyoming, Montana, Colorado, New Mexico and the Sonora Desert in Old Mexico. Andy had also wrangled horses for a large hunting camp in Alaska. His primary guiding expertise was in elk, deer, antelope and sheep. Like many other guides in this part of the country, Andy was well versed in the moods of the grizzly bears and had accumulated an entertaining list of stories about personal encounters over his years of guiding.

Andy made three trips to the Antarctic to work at McMurdo Station. His first time at McMurdo was for a full year. The other two assignments were summer seasons October through February. McMurdo is one of the most isolated communities on the planet.

I first made contact with Andy through an ad I had placed in the *Trapper & Predator Caller* magazine. A trapper from Cody, Wyoming, answered the ad and I contacted him. As it turned out Ross Welfl was unable to accept the position but he recommended Andy as a person who might qualify for the job. He told me that Andy was not a trapper but was a highly skilled guide working out of Cody and that he might be interested. I contacted Andy, talked to him about his qualifications, and immediately put him on my list of possible employees for the 1996 season. A month or so later I went to the Sportsman Show in Portland and talked to some guiding outfits from Wyoming. I asked them if they had ever heard of Andy Johnson and it turned out that he had worked for a couple of them. The ones that he hadn't worked for knew of his sterling reputation. Everyone I talked to about Andy recommended him highly. In the early months of 1996 after a few calls to Andy's references, I flew out to Cody and spent a few days getting to know him.

During my stay we made the rounds of Cody, meeting some of the guides who were holed up for the winter, and a few of Andy's friends, including Randy Blackburn, a well-known local guide and trapper. We also did a little horn hunting and attended some local events. It didn't take long for me to make up my mind to hire Andy and it was one of the best decisions I ever made.

After six years of seasonal work trapping bears on timber company contracts in Oregon, Andy applied for and was successful in getting a job with the Wyoming Game and Fish Department. He ended up working for several seasons capturing problem grizzly and black bears under the direction of Mark Bruscino out of the Cody office.

Since his bear nuisance control work, Andy has continued to use his considerable outdoor and wildlife skills in several other endeavors, including wintertime trapping/monitoring of wolverine in and around Yellowstone National Park, and monitoring of bighorn sheep for Wyoming Game and Fish. Andy is currently assisting in the monitoring of wolves around the Yellowstone country for the Wyoming Game and Fish Department.

Even though Andy was a well-known and highly respected professional guide, I found out that even he could occasionally forget where he was. After years of working in the Rocky Mountains where his compass was his continual trusted companion, Andy was rarely confused about direction. When Andy came to work for me, his work district was bordered on the west side by the Pacific Ocean. On one occasion right after Andy first arrived, he treated me to one of those comical moments in life that I will never forget.

We were on the high rugged west slope of Onion Peak in the northwest corner of Oregon on a seldom used old logging road that snaked around the side of the mountain and dropped off in a near cliff below us. We could clearly see the little community of Cannon Beach far below where Highway 101 runs up the coast toward Seaside. The Pacific Ocean stretched out to the far horizon.

Andy was new to the area and bear damage so I was filling him in on his responsibilities. We stopped to look off into a little canyon with some bear-peeled trees that were turning red from being peeled the previous year. I was glassing this little canyon on the east side of the ridge where we were parked. When I turned around there was Andy, the seasoned top-hand guide with years of professional experience, having worked for some of the best outfitters in Wyoming, looking intently into his palm where his trusty compass nestled. From where Andy stood he was sky-lined, the wide blue Pacific Ocean the only object between him and Japan!

I must have had a startled look on my face when Andy looked up because the light went on for him. He looked like a small boy with his hand caught in the cookie jar and we both had a good laugh. Of course, I told him I would never let him forget that little slip and I always like to live up to my promises. A lesson I learned the hard way, early in my contracting career.

Andy ended up working with me for six seasons and his quality of work was exceptional. Not only did I hire a great employee but I ended up with a first-class lifelong friend. Like with several of my other employees over the years, it is safe to say that I learned more from Andy than he did from me. Andy and his wife, Ali, live on a small ranch in the Burlington area of Wyoming.

Denny Schutz

Denny Schutz was one of my all-time favorite employees! Not that we didn't have our differences (it was a roller coaster ride with Denny as an employee), but I never met a harder worker or more big hearted person! Denny also has a sense of humor that is matched by few people I have met in my lifetime. I asked Denny to give me a little information about his life as a trapper, and in his usual thorough style he gave me some good information and infused a little humor that maybe only trappers can appreciate. Like when he made the big move from South Dakota to Montana in order to catch some of those two-hundred-fifty-dollar coyotes, but he could only catch sixty-dollar coyotes!

Dennis J. Schutz was born October 10, 1947, in Eau Claire, Wisconsin, into a family that included a long line of dedicated hunters and trappers. Denny grew up trapping with his family, including Uncle Frank Broskuski, a top bounty fox trapper in Buffalo and Trempelo counties. Two other uncles, Herman and Hubert Schneiders, were both longline mink trappers. Denny started out skinning mink for Uncle Herman on weekends and got to keep the rats and coon for his skinning labor. Later on Denny also did some bounty trapping for fox but, as he put it, "did not get many."

At age 18, Denny joined the U.S. Marine Corps and spent thirteen months in infantry. He proudly served in the Weapons Section, 3rd Platoon, Company I, 3rd Battalion, 7th Marine Regiment, 1st Marine Division in Vietnam. After returning home Denny went to school for a while then dropped out of college and worked several different jobs "to support his trapping habit." In 1968 he married his wife, Jane, who I am sure has proven herself a saint!

Over his long career as a trapper Denny became an accomplished all-around trapper and concentrated primarily on bobcats, coyotes, coon, mink, muskrats, and marten and, of course, those tree peeling bruins in Oregon.

Denny came to work for Gilman's Forest Management in 1995 and continued capturing tree peeling bears for timber company contracts until 2000. When I first met Denny and Jane in Stevensville, Montana, I spent a few days with them, so Denny and I could get to know one another before Denny came to work for me in Oregon that spring. Jane took me aside at one point and told me that Denny could be a little difficult to work with at times, since few employers could live up to his expectations. Jane was right, and I had a difficult time living up to Denny's standards. Nevertheless, I never regretted hiring Denny. He is a one-of-a-kind trapper's trapper. I have met very few people as dedicated to purpose, and none that was harder working than Denny Schutz.

Dean Bartz

Dean was born in Charles City, Iowa, December 26, 1963. He started trapping when he was about nine years old, catching mice and rats for twenty-five and thirty-five cents each. Like many other young would-be trappers, Dean found an old *Fur-Fish-Game* magazine and that was his first inspiration to learn about trapping. Dean's grandfather had a few old traps and, through reading, Dean taught himself to trap the local muskrats. A local guy took him trapping a time or two but mostly he learned about trapping through his own hard work and determination.

Dean first attended a National Trappers Association (NTA) Convention in Marshalltown, Iowa, in 1981. When he was twenty-four years old Dean started working for Rich Reagan, president of the Iowa Trappers Association and a local fur buyer. He spent nine years skinning and scraping coon, fox and coyotes. It was then that he started meeting other trappers and going to state trapping conventions. Trapping demos were a big part of Dean's early education.

Dean started longlining for coons in 1981 in Iowa. That same season he trapped beaver with Dale Bilingsly in his first out-of-state adventure in Arkansas. In the following years Dean trapped for several different hunting clubs in Mississippi, including some well-known properties like Mossy Oak.

By the time Dean started working for me as a bear trapper, he had trapped in nine different states, including Arkansas, Mississippi, Louisiana, Alabama, Maryland, Montana, Wyoming, Texas and Iowa.

Along with his multi-state fur trapping, Dean has done bear control for private timber companies in Oregon, beaver control for timber companies in Arkansas, and feral hog control in several southern states. He also trapped coyotes in the Willamette Valley of Oregon for some of the largest sheep producers of that area. Dean also spent eighteen fall hunting seasons with a bear hunting outfitter in Northern Minnesota.

Dean has made some great coon catches in Iowa and his best catch was 322 in eleven days while trapping alone. He also caught 550 with partner and lifelong friend Matt Lumley in ten days. Another record for Dean was catching over one hundred coons in twenty-four hours with a partner on two different occasions. All the catches Dean made were while he or he and his partner were doing all the skinning. Dean has rubbed shoulders with many of the top trappers in the United States and is a friend of most everyone he meets.

It was a lucky day for me when I accidentally met up with Dean Bartz at a Montana Trappers Association convention in 1995. Since that time Dean and I have trapped together for bears doing timber damage, trapped coyotes for Willamette Valley sheep producers, caught bobcats in the Oregon Cascades and become good friends. In our spare time we have also dug a lot of razor clams together.

Terry Sawyer

Terry was born in 1945 in Walla Walla, Washington, and moved to Embler, Oregon, in 1946. From there Terry's family moved to Prineville when he was eleven years old. Terry grew up around Prineville and then moved to Mitchell where he lived for twenty-three years before moving back to Prineville.

When Terry was in the fourth grade he wrote a story about wanting to be a mink trapper. Terry certainly reached that goal and has been successful at capturing any furbearer he set out to catch. Terry's career started at seven years old trapping for muskrats.

I first remember meeting Terry at an Oregon trappers fur sale at the little Powell Butte Grange Hall just east of Redmond in about 1973. The amount and quality of his bobcats and other furs were impressive. Well over thirty years later his catches and the quality of furs that he handles remain the envy of many Oregon trappers.

I would ratc Terry Sawyer as one of the best cat trappers in eastern Oregon. Terry has run extensive traplines in Arizona, New Mexico, Washington and Oregon. His longest out-of-state run was thirteen consecutive years of trapping in Arizona.

One of Terry's passions in life for many years has been elk hunting and he has rarely failed to fill his tag in the past fifty years. As you might expect from a friend of Van Houston, Terry also enjoys tracking and has taken many elk by that method. Like quite a few of the best trappers I know, Terry doesn't talk much about numbers, no matter if it concerns hunting or trapping. He knows the futility of comparing skills based on numbers alone.

For nearly twenty years Terry made a substantial part of his livelihood working as a river guide on the John Day and Deshutes rivers. He also worked seasonally for the Bureau of Land Management (BLM) for fourteen years doing firefighting and operating heavy equipment. Terry also contracted one year to trap coyotes for Wheeler County, doing livestock protection.

I had wanted to hire Terry for bear work for many years, and finally in 2006 I talked him into working for me in the bear damage control business. Terry worked both on the Oregon coast near Astoria and in the Cascades of Lane County during his several seasons as a bear trapper between 2006 and 2013. With his easy-going confident manner, Terry is always a pleasure to work around and he does efficient, high quality work. Like all the other trappers in these short sketches, I consider Terry a lifelong friend.

David Vann

I first remember getting to know Dave Vann around the seventh or eighth grade at the Cottage Grove school that we both attended. By early high school we had become friends primarily through our mutual friendship with Cliff McKillop. A group of us young guys would gather in study hall and discuss trapping on a regular basis. I remember Dave, Cliff, Mike Bush, Byron Stone, and myself being a part of those many strategy sessions and sharing the small amount of trapping or hunting information we had at the time. Dave and I stayed in contact over the years as he worked as a logger and trapped every season on the side. Over the years our friendship grew and we eventually trapped together for marten in the Cascades and camped together at our Summer Lake muskrat camp.

Dave spent his entire working career as a logger and before his retirement was well known as one of the top shovel operators at loading log trucks in western Oregon. Like many loggers, his entire world revolved around the outdoors. Family, hunting, fishing and trapping were always his highest priorities in life. Dave's abilities as a blacktail buck hunter are not known to many but have been matched by few. He is also an avid fisherman and makes good use of his skills. When it came to trapping, Dave was highly competitive and we always had a lot of fun arguing about who was the best trapper. Whenever we trapped together Dave always claimed to catch more than I, especially when it came to marten and muskrats. I am pretty sure that sometimes he was lying just to see how hard he could make me work! He was successful in that attempt and I would work twice as hard to out-catch him. However, no matter how hard I worked, he always had a higher catch than I. I just couldn't figure it out.

Dave was an excellent and innovative employee and trapper. His development of our bear bait system saved untold hours of hard work carrying large baits to our bear sets, not to mention the cost of purchasing, transporting and storing of up to 500 beaver carcasses, beef head or sheep skins to use as bear bait each spring. Dave is also one of the most generous people I have ever known. One of his greatest gifts was spending time with and doing things for many of the old-timers who couldn't get around on their own any longer.

Dave worked for me off and on for a number of years in a variety of areas and did a great job wherever he was stationed. His only real weakness was his inability to read a map and stay within certain boundary lines. Like my friend Joe Colver, I found it necessary to keep Dave on a tight line when it came to property boundaries. Dave taught me a lot of things over the years, but I must admit that he taught me more about marten trapping in a few days than I had put together in accumulated knowledge in twenty-five years of running my own marten lines. Friends like Dave are difficult to come by. Even though Dave earned a regular check through our company for awhile, I never considered him an employee but only as a lifelong friend.

David Walp

Many of the trappers who worked with me over the nearly thirty years of my contracting for bear damage and other animal damage control were highly skilled at their chosen trade. During that same general time period, the radical animal rights extremists have waged a relentless campaign to invent in the mind of the general public a caricature of what they believe a trapper really is. This Brutus-like, mean, uneducated troll is not at all what I have known in a lifetime of working with and knowing many trappers personally.

The trappers working for me doing professional wildlife control have had worthy personal qualities and exceptional outdoor skills. In Dave Walp's case I would like to give a few extra details because he is a good example of the varied skills and good qualities that many of these trappers possess. To be sure, trappers are not perfect or without flaws. However, the vast majority of them are good hard-working, family oriented and honest people.

 David Walp was born December 6, 1941, in Portland, and in just a few years his family settled near the beautiful McKenzie River where Dave has lived his entire life. Dave worked for me for two bear seasons and has been a trapper for more than sixty years.

Dave worked for many years as a river guide for the well-known Helfrich Family, a guiding operation that was started by the legendary river guide and trapper, Prince Helfrich. Dave did his first river trip with Prince when he was just fifteen years old, learning many skills from the old master. Prince Helfrich and his guides were the first to run Idaho's Middle Fork of the Salmon River in wooden drift boats. Few guides have mastered the skills necessary to navigate the Middle Fork in wooden drift boats, and to this day the only guides running hard boats on the Middle Fork of the Salmon are from Oregon.

Dave has continued running wild rivers for more than forty years. During his river guiding days he regularly ran his drift boats on the McKenzie, Rogue, Deschutes and John Day rivers in Oregon, and on some occasions also ran the Blackwater in British Columbia and the Salmon River in Idaho.

Dave has trapped and been a river guide from an early age and, like most other trappers and guides, he has done a variety of other jobs. Earlier in life he worked in the woods logging, worked in sawmills, and was part of a powder crew (powder monkey) during the building of Cougar Dam. Later on, Dave was a chief instructor and program director for the Northwest Outward Bound School for nearly ten years. Dave also worked as a Lane County Deputy Sheriff for fourteen years. During much of that time he was in charge of the boat patrol and worked in search and rescue.

For the past thirty-seven years Dave has taught snowshoeing for the Eugene Parks and Recreation Department's Outdoor Program. He continues to do volunteer work for the Oregon Department of Fish and Wildlife and has done volunteer work for a number of environmental education groups.

It was a good day for me when I hailed Dave as he floated down the Siuslaw River one day in the late winter of 1979. I have counted him as a good friend ever since. I like to think that I have soaked up just a few of the many high qualities and skills of Dave and the other fine trappers and outdoorsmen I have had the privilege to work with and learn from over the past thirty years.

Joe Colver

Joe trapped beaver with the tough old former state beaver trapper Dave Conn and went on to become one of Oregon's best beaver trappers. Like several others of the bear trappers, Joe and I go back to the early 1970s. When the old Oregon Game Commission was headquartered in Portland, Joe spent a tremendous amount of his own time representing trappers in a very positive way. Joe did a lot of good things for trappers and didn't get much credit. I would like to thank him and give him credit for a job well done. Joe worked for me doing bear control for many years. He was highly skilled, dependable and as self-reliant as anyone I ever worked with.

One example of Joe's self-reliance came when Joe was working for me doing bear damage control in the Tillamook State Forest. Joe was snaring bears in the extensive tree damage on the upper Kilches River far back in the old Tillamook Burn.

Joe always drove an International Scout and just kept rebuilding the same old Scout all the years that I knew him. On this particular trap check, Joe broke a front spring support far back in the mountains with no one around for miles. Late Friday afternoon Joe walked for over ten miles to get to the upper Nestucca River at nearly dark. From there he caught a ride to Tillamook and then hitchhiked up Highway 6 and made his way to Portland by about midnight. For those who don't have a map of this area, that little hitchhiking trip was well over one hundred miles.

When Joe reached home he gathered up a mobile welder and parts to fix his Scout. Joe bought and sold Scout parts for years so he had enough parts on hand to build a new Scout if needed. After gathering up the parts and equipment to fix his rig, Joe called a friend and they departed in the wee hours of the morning for the Tillamook Burn. By daylight Joe had his Scout fixed and was back on the road

236

Joe Colver, my friend since the early 1970s, with a pile of beaver pelts.

to continue checking his bear snares. I didn't even hear about this event till a month after it happened. This illustration of dependability is just one example of not only the self-reliance and dedication that many trappers have to checking traps, but also of their ability, like farmers, ranchers and loggers, to fix almost anything in an emergency. Come to think of it, many trappers are farmers, ranchers and loggers.

Joe also had a special way of making coffee that I found remarkable. One year I went down to Joe's camp in the mountains near Garibaldi, where he resided during the bear season for several spring snaring jobs. We got back to camp after a long day of checking bear snares and started to fix ourselves some supper. I noticed on the counter behind the sink of Joe's little camper a row of one quart fruit jars that looked to me like they were full of motor oil.

I asked Joe what was in the jars and he told me it was his coffee. He said he made up a month's supply at home and all he had to do was warm it up while he was camped out. He claimed it was just the same as fresh coffee as long as you don't boil it when heating it up. I had to disagree somewhat with Joe's theory on coffee since I have often tasted it.

Joe was one of those characters I mentioned earlier. As a mechanic he knew everything there was to know about International Scouts, and used that knowledge not only to make a living in the off-season but also to repair and drive the same Scout for nearly all the years that I knew him. That old rig just kept morphing into something different with a constant stream of new engines, fenders, transmissions, rear ends, winches, seats and entire bodies.

Joe was what you would call a dyed-in-the-wool beaver trapper and for most of his life there wasn't anything he would rather do than harvest beavers. Joe could skin, stretch and flesh beaver pelts at the highest levels of quality, and few others could do them so well. Joe's father was a well-to-do doctor in Oregon, and Joe could have easily done many other things in life yet he chose to live a free life as a trapper. Having Joe for an employee was like fighting a Chinook salmon running downstream through the rapids with a hundred yards of line out. He was a constant runaway but you always knew you had something special at the end of the line!

I could write about several other master trappers whom I have known or worked with over the years, but it is a long list and I must stop some place. I will mention my good friend, Ray Jordan, from Joseph, originally from Kentucky. Ray is a great guy to work with and a first-class trapper. It was a privilege to work with Ray and all the bear trappers. They are all highly-skilled, self-motivated, self-reliant individuals. I learned from each one of them and will always treasure the friendships I made over the last fifty-plus years of fur and animal damage control trapping. When someone talks about a trapper with disdain and disparages them as a group, don't believe it. You will never find a finer group of people than trappers. Those mentioned above are just a small sampling of the many I have known.

Thanks to the many trappers I have worked with since 1980. They have been fine companions, good workers and excellent friends. They contributed to the development of many of the stories told in this book.

The Bear Crew in 1999 (from left around the table): Andy Johnson, Bob Gilman, Sam Gilman, Denny Schutz, Dave Van, Matt Peterson, Paul Carlisle and Joe Colver.

Final Thoughts

In 1822, the Northwest Company Trader Alexander Ross engaged an old voyageur in conversation about his life work. The old man recounted many physical accomplishments of his youth, as was the custom of this braggadocio group of great canoe men and explorers. He also recounted many of the rewards of the lifestyle that he had chosen and the temporary riches that he had gained, but quickly lost in the pursuit of extending the enjoyments of life.

The old voyageur then admitted that a large sum of money had passed through his hands and,

> *...although now I have not a spare shirt to my back, nor a penny to buy one. Yet were I young again, I should glory in commencing the same career again, I would willingly spend another half-century in the same fields of enjoyment. There is no life so happy as a voyageur's life; none so independent; no place where a man enjoys so much variety and freedom.*
> *Caesars of the Wilderness*, Peter C. Newman, Viking, 1989, pages 48-49.

In the stories of this book, I have recounted some of the events of my life work as a trapper and the times of enjoyment as a hunter. Trappers and hunters like myself have much in common with this old voyageur. We love what we do, and no matter how difficult the work or how bad the weather, it never seems like work. There are rewards along the trail of life we have chosen, but they are rarely financial. And even though money is necessary to survival, that is not what motivates trappers. The real message of the trapper's life and the thread that links us as a group is in the final words of the old voyageur: "None so independent; no place where a man enjoys so much variety and freedom."

I agree with the voyageur and conclude, after more than fifty years as a trapper, that there is no life that brings more happiness, there is no life more independent, and there is no other place where a man enjoys so much variety and freedom.

Throughout this book, I have proudly used the title "trapper" to identify who I am. Like many other professions, including loggers, miners and cowboys, trappers have a long and proud heritage.

I am a trapper, and I hope that this book at least partially explains what that means.

Ecclesiastes 9:10:
Whatsoever thy hand findeth to do, do it with all thy might.

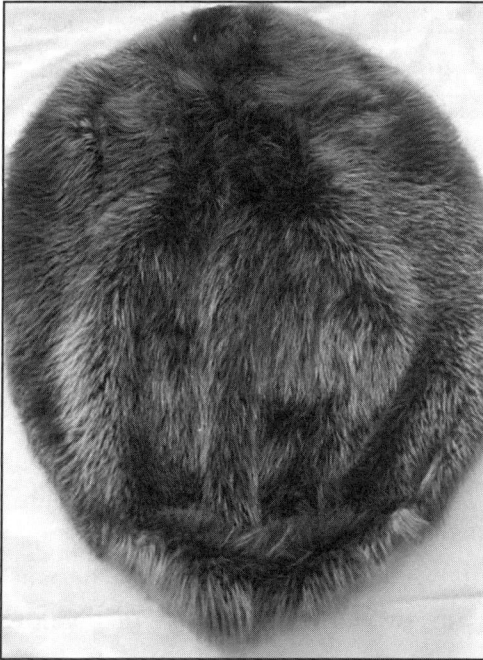

The Author

Bob Gilman started trapping in 1961 at eleven years of age and has since trapped, hunted and fished over a wide area of Oregon on both the west and east sides of the Cascade Mountains.

From 1976 through 1986, he trapped for furs to earn a major portion of his family's livelihood. In 1980 he began contract work for private companies and individuals doing mountain beaver, river beaver, and other wildlife damage control trapping.

In 1986 Bob began work for the U.S. Fish and Wildlife Service doing seasonal bear damage control work and in 1988 started contracting privately. In the last twenty-eight years, he has contracted for a cooperative of timberland managers that has included many of the largest land ownerships in Oregon. Bob has also contracted with Oregon State University and the Oregon Department of Fish and Wildlife to capture bears on two telemetry studies and with the Department of Fish and Wildlife to capture martens for study.

Bob has served as an officer in the Oregon Trappers Association for many years. He is currently Oregon Director for the National Trappers Association. He was inducted into the Oregon Trappers Hall of Fame by his peers in 2012.

Bob still works full-time doing animal damage control and continues to do forestry, farm, ranch and rural work. Much of the current demand for his services also comes from city dwellers where skunks, squirrels, raccoons, nutria, coyotes and other wildlife do extensive and costly damage to homes, businesses and government properties.

His favorite pastimes are hunting, fishing and camping with family and friends. Bob has actively served in his local church for the past thirty-five years. Bob has been married to his wife, Judy, for forty-six years, has two children and six grandchildren.

Bob Gilman with a bear-peeled tree

Bibliography

Blackburn, Randy and Bob Hamilton. *Your Guided Hunt and What You Should Know*. Wyoming: Randy Blackburn, 1996.

Brimlow, George Francis. *Harney County Oregon and its Range Land*. Binfords & Mort, 1951.

Brogan, Phil F. *East of the Cascades*. Binford & Mort, 1976.

Brown, Wilfred. *Tin Pot Valley*. Wilfred Brown, Drain, Oregon.

Dailey, E.J. *Traplines and Trails*. Read Books, 2008.

Douglas, David and John Davies. *Douglas of the Forest: The North American Journals of David Douglas*. P. Harris, 1979.

Ellis, Lucia. *Tillamook Burn Country: A Pictorial History*. Caxton Printers, 1983.

Fisher, Jim. *Starker Forests: The Legacy of T.J. Starker*. Starker Forests, Inc., 1991.

Flowers, Ralph. *Bears and Flowers*. Ralph Flowers, 2003.

Flowers, Ralph. *The Education of a Bear Hunter.* Binford & Mort, 1989.

Harding, A. *Deadfalls and Snares: A Book of Instruction for Trappers about Snares and other Home-Made Traps*. LULU Press, 2010.

Keil, Bill. "One Survived While Others Died." *Sports Afield*. Jan. 1992

McManus, Patrick F. *The Grasshopper Trap*. New York: Owl Books, 1989.

Minter A. Harold, *Umpqua Valley Oregon and its Pioneers*. Binford & Mort, 1967.

Mitchell, Ann Lindsay, Syd House. *David Douglas: Explorer and Botanist*. Aurum Press, Ltd., 1999.

Negus, Wayne. *Wilderness Tales and Trails*. Negus, 1990.

Newman, Peter C. *Caesars of the Wilderness*, Viking, 1987.

O'Hearn, Seales Nancy, Edwards, Patricia Ann and Hing, Marna Lee. *Sawdust & Cider: A History of Lorane, Oregon and the Siuslaw Valley.* Maverick Publications, 1987.

Rezendes, Paul. *Tracking & the Art of Seeing: How to Read Animal Tracks and Sign.* New York: Harper Collins, 1999.

Thoele, Michael and Ron Brentano. *Bohemia: The Lives and Times of an Oregon Timber Venture.* Portland: Oregon Historical Society Press, 1998.

Webber, Burt and Margie Webber. *This Was Logging and Sawmilling (Books About the Oregon Country).* Web Research Group, 1996.

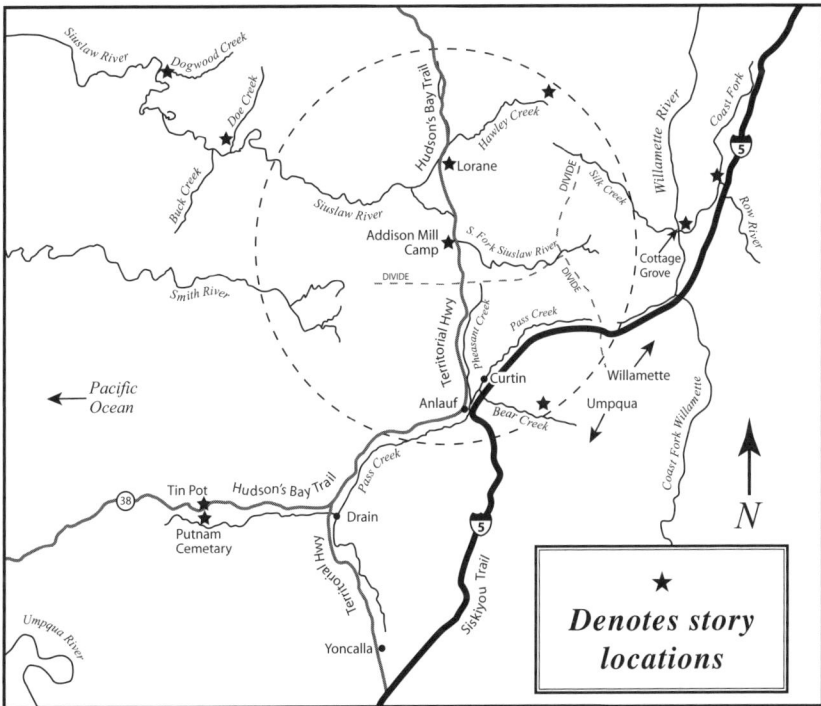

★ Denotes story locations